THE

SPECIAL

CHOSEN

ONE

The Special Chosen One © 2013 by Susan Beckman. All Rights Reserved

No portion of this book may be copied, retransmitted, reposted, duplicated, or otherwise used without the express written approval of the author, except by reviewers who may quote brief excerpts in connection with a review. Any unauthorized copying, reproduction, translation, or distribution of any part of this material without permission by the author is prohibited and against the law.

Disclaimer and Terms of Use: No information contained in this book should be considered as legal advice. Reliance upon information and content obtained through this book is solely at the reader's own risk. The author assumes no liability or responsibility for damage or injury to the reader, other persons or property arising from any use of any product, information, idea or instruction contained in the content through this book. Reliance upon information contained in this material is solely at the reader's own risk. The author has no financial interest in and receives no compensation from manufacturers of products or websites mentioned.

This book is designed to provide general information regarding the subject matter covered. However, rules, regulations, laws, practices, and the interpretation of same often change or vary from state to state, country to country, and agency to agency. Because each situation is different, the reader is advised to consult with his or her own advisor regarding that individual's specific situation.

Neither the author nor the publisher assume any responsibility for any errors or omissions, nor do they represent or warrant that the information, ideas, plans, actions, suggestions, and methods of operation contained herein is in all cases true, accurate, appropriate, or legal. It is the reader's responsibility to consult with his or her own advisor before putting any of the enclosed information, ideas, or practices into play. The author specifically disclaims any liability resulting from the use or application of the information contained in this book, and the information is not intended to serve as legal advice related to individual situations.

This book is a true story of the author's experience and research. Some names have been changed to protect the individual's identity.

sbeckmanauthor@aol.com

Library of Congress Cataloging-in-Publication Data HQ755.7-759.92

ISBN-13: 978-0-9911767-1-7
ISBN-10: 0991176715
eBook: 978-0-9911767-2-4

The Special Chosen One Photographs © 2013 by Greg Beckman

Printed in the United States of America

Praise for The Special Chosen One

Have you ever wondered how it feels to be an adoptee; to be a young child and wonder why your "real" mom and dad gave you away? Can you imagine the feeling of being scared to death to talk to your adoptive parents about it because they might get angry or be hurt? Susan Beckman has captured the feelings of most adoptees whose entire identities have been locked up in a sealed record FOREVER. There are no words to adequately describe how eloquently the author captures the events and feelings of being a "Special Chosen Child" and the burden that connotation carries as she seeks to find the answer WHY - it is the one question that haunts most adoptees! It is a riveting book and difficult to put down. This book should be read by all, but especially by every adoptive parent!

—Sandy Musser, Author & Adoption Activist
-Founder of: ALARM, ATM,
Adoption & Family Reunion Center
-Author of: *I Would Have Searched Forever*
What Kind of Love is This?
To Prison with Love

As a Coordinator of The Alma Society, and a member for more than 22 years, and as an adoptee, it is without hesitation that I endorse Susan Beckman's book, *The Special Chosen One, An Adopted Woman's Journey Back to her Roots*. It should be read by all members of the adoption triad, and in particular, by adoptees. Susan shares her story of looking for her birth parents following some of the guiding principles of research provided by The Alma Society, and she also shares with the reader her very own qualms about how she feels about searching and the effect it has on her own life, her own family, and that of her adoptive parents. It's a page turner - and the reader will understand why the adoptee always has the question of "Why?"

—Marie H. Anderson, Coordinator
The ALMA Society
www.almasociety.org
P. O. Box 85
Denville, NJ 07834

As the Executive Director of Crystal Adoptions, an Adoption Advisor and a mother and grandmother, I am happy to endorse Susan Beckman's book, *The Special Chosen One, An Adopted Woman's Journey Back to her Roots*. I was especially touched by Susan's memories of what she was feeling as an adopted child; sometimes feelings we don't even imagine as the adults in an adopted child's life and things that eventually influence the perception we have of adoption in adulthood. I found this book moving yet informative and an easy read and will definitely recommend it to my clients as they prepare for adoption.

—R. Dee Waltz-Shihady, Executive Director
Crystal Adoptions
Twitter: @Helping_U_Adopt
Web page: www.CrystalAdoptions.com
LinkedIn: Crystal Adoptions on LinkedIn

I couldn't put this book down and read it in one day. Absolutely Gripping. As a father of adopted children I found myself deeply moved as Susan's story allows the reader to peer into the mind and emotions of a child who wonders about their birth parents. Susan also shares keen and helpful insights into the tension between loving her adoptive parents and at the same time wanting to have a relationship with her birth parents. For those who are adopted, Susan brings a sense of healing in knowing that you are not alone. This book is a must read for anyone who is adopted, has adopted, thinking of adoption or in the process of adopting.

—Dan Plourde, MS
Pastor, Calvary Chapel

Foreward

⌒⤫

Have you ever felt something missing? Ever felt if you were able to look just this way or that way at a slightly different angle you would see just who you were supposed to be?

The Special Chosen One takes us on such a journey. Well...several distinct and yet complete journeys.

Susan knew at the age of six something was missing. A tooth was missing from a gear. The screen of her life didn't quite cover the window. And for more than 40 years she searched for truth.

This is a story relatively unknown by those of us who have no adoption in our families. Yes, we all know folks who have been adopted. But we know little of their struggles, both emotional and psychological.

Susan Beckman has written a small masterpiece. It is at once accessible, and full of love and self-deprecating humor. It will give all who read it a simple peace and leave them smiling. It is an entree of sorts into a world heretofore unknown.

I was thrilled that she got busted by her Mom knowing that she had been through all this behind her back…because Moms know everything!

It is a book you will be tempted to start at bedtime. But, regrettably one which you will be loath to put down, making you late for or at least groggy at work.

Therefore, I recommend you put aside the time, say on a rainy Saturday afternoon, as I did, and read it through. You will not be sorry.

—Lar Sinclair

Am I Special because I'm Chosen?

Or was I Chosen because I'm Special?

CONTENTS

Chapter 1	What's Wrong With You?	1
Chapter 2	The One	9
Chapter 3	Chosen Brother	13
Chapter 4	Miracle Sister	23
Chapter 5	Lies	31
Chapter 6	The Question	43
Chapter 7	The Move	47
Chapter 8	Toes	55
Chapter 9	Does Anyone Know?	61
Chapter 10	Cheeseburger & Fries Confession	69
Chapter 11	I Don't Know	73
Chapter 12	I'm Not Interested	81
Chapter 13	The Brown Metal Box	89
Chapter 14	Tear-Stained Letter	99
Chapter 15	The Delivery Room	107
Chapter 16	The Dangling Page	113
Chapter 17	Three-Foot Long Drawers	123
Chapter 18	Deer Hunting	133
Chapter 19	Your Cheatin' Heart	141
Chapter 20	Covering the Bases	151
Chapter 21	Loretta Lynn	157

Chapter 22	Pulled Apart	163
Chapter 23	California Here We Come	171
Chapter 24	The Soda Pop Joint	183
Chapter 25	Less Than Nine Months	189
Chapter 26	Please Don't Hang Up	201
Chapter 27	Did You Pay?	207
Chapter 28	Dundee Bar & Lounge	217
Chapter 29	Saying Good-Bye	225
Chapter 30	The End – Or So I Thought	231
Chapter 31	Me	235

Epilogue 237
For Adoptees 241
For Birth Parents...243
For Adoptive Parents 245
Acknowledgments..249
Reading Group Questions 253
Tips To Begin Searching 255
Recommended Reading 257
Helpful Links 265
Photos 269
About the Author 283

This is how I imagined it:

They hold hands as they wander around
a big room with oodles of babies.

With index fingers on their chins,
they ponder their choices.

That one has blonde peach fuzz.
This one has black hair.
Look at that one.

She has long fingers
she'll either be a piano player or a thief.

I think she looks healthy. I wonder if she'll be smart.
Which one looks most like us?

This baby boy looks sickly.
She looks perfect.

I am the one they chose.
They picked me.

I'm special!

And they named me

Susan Marie.

Chapter 1

What's Wrong With You?

Taking a deep breath, I turned the latch and tiptoed inside.

Do I pretend like nothing happened? Or do I spill my guts? Tell them the puzzled thoughts running rampant in my head?

I crept upstairs to my bedroom. I exhaled, only now aware of holding my breath. With raw feelings exposed, I'm destined to be in big trouble now. Wishing I'd kept my mouth shut, I choked back a whimper. I could crawl in bed—stay buried under the covers. No—I wanted to leave, get away from it all.

The mind is a mysterious hidden entity, which conceals a complexity of emotions from one extreme to the other. Random options bounced around in my head, like a ping-pong ball gone wild. I wanted to turn back time and not have caused any of this turmoil.

My mistake. I'm the sinful one.

Instead of chemistry homework, I focused on the radio station playing a Beatles' song, and I am *The Fool on the Hill*, because nobody seemed to like me and I never showed my feelings.

I sat cross-legged on my yellow sunflower bedspread, stared blankly at the clouds, daydreamed, and wanted to jump out the window. I listened to distant thunder and gazed across the wheat field. The wind swayed the tops back and forth like feathers. I wished the wind would whisk me away.

My dad's thunderous voice interrupted my stray visions, "Susan, come down here. Right now!"

They waited for me in the kitchen.

Unable to look at them, knowing what was to come, I absent-mindedly watched the potatoes boil inside the stainless-steel kettle as airy blobs of white foam danced up and down. The steaming pot roast rested in the pan, awaiting the carving knife. The Land O'Lakes butter melted and faded away as kernels of corn swallowed the yellow liquid.

"What's wrong with you? How can you do this?"

No right answer formed in my mind. I didn't know what they wanted to hear.

His closed fist slammed on the wooden kitchen table. "Aren't you thankful for everything we've done? Answer me! What's wrong with you?"

+ + +

I set the ball rolling three days earlier. The high school guidance counselor, Mrs. Shart, listened to my distress. My tangled fairy-tale fantasies tumbled around, like a hamster running in a wheel which never stops spinning and never gets anywhere.

Like most teenagers floundering in the 1970s, I tried to find myself. But how could I find myself when I didn't even know where I came from?

My heart unlocked. I released 15 years of pent-up heartache.

"My adoptive parents named me Susan Marie. My birth mother was 17, my birth father 18 and they both had very high IQs. That's all I know. And I want to find them."

"Have you talked to your parents about this?"

"That's the problem. They won't talk about it. I don't want to hurt them. They're my parents. I don't want to replace them, either. I just want to know who my birth parents are. But I can't ask."

"Would you like me to talk to your mother?"

"Yes," I whispered, and questioned whether I made the right decision. If it was the wrong decision, I wasn't prepared to pay the price.

The day approached when the counselor planned on calling my mom to school, but I didn't tell anyone. I remained fidgety and avoided eye contact with my mom before I left that morning. I couldn't focus in my classes, waiting to hear the result of their meeting.

Summoned out of algebra class to the counselor's office, I walked in front of the classroom and opened the door.

This is embarrassing. They're all gonna gawk and wonder what I did wrong.

I stepped into the hall and closed the door behind me.

CLICK.

Placing one foot in front of the other, I trudged along like a death-row inmate headed toward my execution. At least I wouldn't be the one to tell my mom. My parents won't be mad at me now...I hoped.

The beige, metal lockers seemed like they closed in on both sides of me as I advanced through another hallway. A faint odor of burnt wood briefly drifted past my nose as I passed the wood shop class.

I trusted Mrs. Shart wouldn't allow my mom to get mad. She's the guidance counselor. Her job is to guide and counsel, isn't it? She won't let anything bad happen.

I stepped into the office. My mom sat on the edge of a heavy wood chair, both hands clenched around the fake brown-leather purse in her lap, lips clamped together, her back as straight as a rod. I didn't expect this.

Heat rose to my neck and onto my face. An unexpected stabbing pain in my right temple mushroomed inside my head, like a sizzling firecracker waiting to blow up. I swallowed the bitter sour liquid which flooded my mouth.

The hairline crack between the floor tiles

jumped at me.

Step on a crack, break your mother's back.

If I tapped my toe on the crack, without getting caught, and her back really broke, she'd forget about this whole nightmare. She'd be in the hospital more worried about her broken back than my obsessive fantasy to find my birth parents.

I avoided my mom's scowling expression. Waves of guilt engulfed me—guilty of what, I didn't know.

"We'll talk about this later when you get home, Susan."

I frowned at Mrs. Shart for a split second. I trusted her. With her head tilted, she wrinkled her forehead. The look in her eyes said *I'm sorry*. But she didn't know what I faced when I got home.

Turn. Run—that's what I wanted to do. Run far, far away—away from school, away from home, away from my parents—away from myself. Where I wanted to run to, I didn't know. I simply wanted to get away.

Another explosive bang of his fist startled

me back to reality as I flinched. Shivers crawled up my spine. The ashes from the tip of his Winston cigarette missed the ashtray and landed on the table.

"What is wrong with you? Why do you want to find your real mother anyway."

"I want to know who she is, where I came from."

I stood anchored to the linoleum floor. How should I answer his questions? What did he want me to say?

"I don't want to replace you guys. You're my parents."

"Then what's wrong with you? Huh? Answer me!"

I caught sight of dessert: a pineapple upside-down cake, with maraschino cherries meticulously aligned in the center hole of each pineapple slice, whole pecans in between, a blanket of gooey brown-sugar syrup oozed over the sides onto the silver platter.

"What – is – wrong – with – you?"

In a whisper I said, "I don't know."

"We are your parents. You should be thankful. I don't want to hear any more of this talk about looking for your real mother. Do you understand me?"

"Yes, Daddy."

Back in my bedroom I wondered, what in the world *was* really wrong with me, as the radio played *I Wish It Would Rain*, by The Temptations, singing about a face against the window pane, and no one will know I'm crying because the raindrops will hide my teardrops.

Chapter 2

The One

My life began August 9, 1954, although I was born on July 18, 1954.

Where had I slept during the three weeks after my birth?

Nobody knew.
Nobody wanted to know.
Nobody cared.

Or at least nobody talked.

I never knew another mother or father.

I don't remember a moment when I did *not* know I was adopted or when first told of my adoption, a detail never concealed. It became a natural part of my life, enmeshed into my spirit. A fact I always knew. No big deal—as a youngster.

But also a subject not openly discussed in our home.

I loved my adoptive parents.

+ + +

That's my Mama; short, curly permed hair and black-rimmed glasses. I whiffed Oriental traces of Emeraude perfume. She pushed the swing higher, as I stretched my legs to touch the clouds with my toes. Read bedtime stories and sewed pretty dresses. She baked luscious rhubarb pies and scooped a dollop of rich vanilla ice cream on top of each warm slice.

My Daddy stood 6 feet 2 inches tall, with a deep, robust voice. He perched me on his shoulders, ran around the yard as I squealed in delight. He hauled jumbo boxes home, from Consolidated Corrugated Box Company where he worked, and carved windows on the sides. They transformed into the right-sized playhouse. His giantic, powerful hands would squeeze the tar out of you with his hugs or inflict the most painful spankings.

+ + +

The One

Every morning I looked in the mirror at my chocolate-brown eyes, brown hair, crooked smile and big nose. *Does anyone live in Michigan who looks like me?*

I considered my nationality. I speculated what blood relative passed on their big nose to me! Italian? No, because my nose isn't *that* big. Maybe Polish; they have big noses, don't they? What about dark hair and eyes? Don't French people have those features?

I'm supposed to be Hungarian, because my Daddy is Hungarian. But I mimicked any kind of ethnic group I desired, dependent upon my mood. I could pretend to be any nationality because, after all, I am The One.

The prison doors of my mind locked in questions which would cause heartbreak and pain.

But you couldn't padlock my eyes.

I am the cunning one who focused on the unfamiliar woman in aisle 10 of Kroger's, the one who flaunted dark hair and brown eyes—and nobody observed my mission.

I am the sneaky one who scrutinized the mannerisms of every person who ate a grilled cheese sandwich at the lunch counter in Woolworth's who displayed a big nose—and nobody noticed.

    I am the one who learned to manipulate my eyes, peeking back over my shoulder, without anyone catching on to my tactics, so I could get one last glimpse of the one who truly might be *her*.

Chapter 3

Chosen Brother

We entered an unfamiliar professional-looking building. No racks of clothes. No toy department. No soda fountain counter. Not the casual atmosphere I was accustomed to at the Five and Dime where we often shopped.

Circular glass doors revolved around, and threw flashes of light across mirror-like marble floors. Brass doorknobs and crystal chandeliers brought forth my best behavior.

The dark-skinned elevator doorman nodded his head, giving me permission to press the number 2 button. My stomach flip-flopped when we ascended to the second floor.

As we exited, my mom grabbed my hand. We paraded along the endless corridor, and passed mahogany doors encased with frosted glass in the upper half, which reminded me of iced-over windows in wintertime.

We stopped at one door that stood ajar, which I later learned was the adoption agency. My mom leaned down and whispered, "Honey, see the nice young man sitting behind the desk?"

"Yes, Mama."

"You go climb on his lap. Tell him how much you want a baby brother."

"Okay, Mama."

My four-year-old charm accomplished the trick. My parents always told me I'm special.

The talk in our house now centered on a baby. No one explained in detail where the baby would come from or how it will get delivered to our home, but I suspected the baby might also be chosen, like me.

+ + +

Driving to the far side of town one chilly day in March 1959, Daddy parked in front of a small, plain one-story house with a sagging, weathered porch. Once-white paint flaked off and exposed patches of bare, rotting wood. A foster home.

Fragments of this scene lingered as a blur in my mind, like a long-ago dream. Children played on the floor, with shades drawn and curtains pulled tight, dim and gloomy.

Behind a splintered wooden door stood a dingy white basket on wheels. Cautiously I slipped through the door, stretched onto my tip-toes and peeked inside—a sleeping baby.

I don't remember leaving the house or riding home with the baby.

My next memory was this baby boy, whom we named Kevin, asleep in a beige wicker clothes basket on top of our console stereo. I climbed on a chair and stretched my neck to peer over the side.

The smell of Johnson's Baby Lotion reminded me of brand-new plastic baby dolls. I stroked the silky blue binding around the blanket and tried to move it enough to wake him, without getting caught by my parents.

Barely six weeks old, I have no idea what I expected him to do.

When he stretched an arm into the air, scrunched his forehead, puckered his lips and grunted, I waited for him to peek at me for an instant.

His arm dropped and became motionless. I watched the blanket ever so slightly rise and fall with each short breath. I waited nearby. When his eyes opened for the first time in our house I wanted to share with him the home I loved.

This is boring. He's gonna sleep forever. I have better things to do.

"Mama, I'm going to LeeAnn's house. Let me know when Kevin wakes up."

"Sure, Honey. But listen for me to call you."

In those days, when parents wanted their children to come home, they opened the outside door, yelled their child's name, and expected them to run home.

I now realize I was not even five years old and my parents let me play outside alone? It sure was a different world back in 1959!

LeeAnn and I sat in the car inside her garage and pretended we were driving, a common pastime for kids back then. Much more fun than sitting at home. When our imaginary driving trip ended, I went home.

My brother was awake. I'm disappointed. "Why didn't you call me?"

"We did, but you didn't come home. Where were you?"

"In LeeAnn's garage, pretend driving. The windows were closed in the car and I didn't hear you."

Months passed as we eased into a daily schedule with a baby in our house.

I attended kindergarten the fall of 1959. The excitement of meeting new friends in school kept me awake at night, along with the fear of abandoning my mom and brother every day. Home was my safe haven. Our routine would be broken.

I loved my baby brother. I didn't want to leave him.

What if someone comes and grabs him during the day and I don't get to say good-bye?

At night my pillowcase soaked up the tears. Brokenhearted in the mornings when I left for school, I returned home every afternoon, swung open the screen door, ran to Kevin and wrapped my arms around him.

We knew we were loved, with kisses and

hugs plentiful in our home. We were a happy family.

+ + +

Life went on. An outsider might not notice we were adopted. We *appeared* to function as normal as our neighbors. We weren't any different. Nothing seemed peculiar or abnormal.

We enjoyed backyard cookouts under the shady maple tree. I roller-skated with neighborhood friends. We played baseball in the street, Red Rover-Red Rover and hide-and-seek, always home at night when the street lights flickered on.

Our moms hung laundry from clotheslines on Mondays, ironed on Tuesdays, cleaned on Wednesdays, grocery shopped on Thursdays and planned weekend activities on Fridays. Our dads worked from 8:00 to 5:00 Monday through Friday, mowed the grass or played golf on Saturdays, and attended church with their families on Sundays.

Our lifestyle perhaps was as typical as any other 1950's All-American family. Adoption didn't *seem* to affect us. We were *almost* a duplicate of other families.

But then again, we never discussed

adoption. The subject was never encouraged. Period.

Did we not talk about adoption to superficially pretend our household wasn't any different from others?

Or did we not talk about adoption because my parents were terrified if the "A" word was spoken, then a real, live birth mother might appear on our doorstep and pose a threat to our perfect little family?

+ + +

One brisk October day, as golden orange-red leaves from the elm trees swirled around, I stayed home from school with tonsillitis. My nine-month-old brother amused himself with toys scattered throughout the living room. I sat on the couch with my own toys.

For the most part, except when company dropped by, a flimsy, gold-fringed cover was draped over the couch.

Mama absorbed herself with daily chores. She hustled through the room and caught sight of a car as it turned into our driveway.

Spying through the curtain, "Oh, my God, the social worker is here. Hurry! Get up!"

She swooped toys from the floor and flung them onto the couch. She scrambled to gather together the four corners of the throw cover, satisfied all the toys laid nestled inside, threw it over her shoulder like Santa Claus, fled to the closet, stuffed it in the corner and slammed the closet door in the nick of time.

DING-DONG.

Paralyzed in the middle of the room, bug-eyed and somewhat confused, I panicked. I wasn't able to utter the words that formed in my head.

What happened? Why hide our toys because the social worker's here? What should I do now? How am I supposed to act?

My mom scooped up my brother, while at the same time commanded me, "Go sit in that chair and *be good*."

"Hello, Mrs. Burrows. Come on in."

Oh, I see. We have company! That's why she took the cover off the couch. But why hide our toys?

The perfect house, with perfect little children and the perfect, uncluttered living room equaled a perfect meeting with the social worker.

If everything was so perfect in our All-American home, why was my mom crying that night? I was supposed to be asleep in bed, but instead crouched on the landing at the top of the stairs, hidden from my parents' view. Parts of their conversation muffled—half of it I didn't understand.

"Rudy, what if they take Kevin away from us?"

"It's okay, Marie. I'm sure it will be all right."

"But what if I wouldn't have gotten all those toys put away in time? What if she would have seen them all over the floor and couch? I moved as fast as I could and jammed them into the closet. I'm sure I scared Susan half to death. I didn't even check the rest of the room to see if anything else was out of place. Ohhhhh...I sure hope she didn't notice the dirty breakfast dishes in the sink."

"Honey, it's okay. I'm sure she wasn't here to see how clean the house was. Don't worry."

"What if she didn't like what she saw? They could take him away, you know, just like that," snapping her fingers. "I'm so worried now. We still have another five months where they can change their mind. I don't know what I'd do if they took him from us."

Tears cascaded over my cheeks, dribbled onto my jammas. My lips tasted salty. I snuck back to our bedroom and gingerly maneuvered around areas that squeaked if stepped on. Kevin slept in his crib.

He doesn't know the danger he's in. Why would someone steal him away from us? Maybe it's like at the foster home. We stepped into their house and took him. Maybe that's how it works—somebody might come into our house and take him away.

My parents never expressed fear of anything. They were the strong, protective ones. They sheltered our perfect little family.

We didn't talk about adoption. We didn't talk about the possibility that someone could snatch us away. We didn't talk to other people about it, either. It wasn't discussed.

Why was it different with our family?

I had no one to talk to. I didn't know anyone who was adopted, except my brother.

But he might not remain my brother much longer.

Chapter 4

Miracle Sister

By Christmas of 1959, my parents chattered about another baby. No hint of special or chosen.

They said, "We're calling this one the *miracle* baby."

At five, I didn't concern myself with details of where this one would come from or what made a miracle baby different from special or chosen. I thrived on the idea of another baby in the house.

In Michigan, during 1959, a birth mother could change her mind within one year. If she wanted her baby back, the adoptive parents had no choice but return it.

My parents still remained within the one-year probationary time period. Three months dangled in the air before my brother's adoption was final. After that, no turning back—for the birth mother or the adoptive parents. No one would be allowed to uproot him then.

But a lot might happen in three months.

I recognized uneasiness with my parents.

The late nights they huddled around the kitchen table in whispered conversations. The wide-eyed, panicked looks cast towards each other when the doorbell rang. Instant suspicion of a cheerful stranger who smiled at my brother in the grocery store. Skeptical when they answered the phone and heard chilling silence.

No social workers popped in to inspect our home for the miracle baby's arrival. They didn't mention plans to pick it up from a stranger's house.

But the atmosphere shifted to something altogether different with this baby. Even though it hadn't appeared yet, something seemed odd. The mood wasn't the same as the time we chose my brother.

"Don't tell anyone about our miracle baby. We want to wait and surprise everyone, so don't say anything to anyone, especially any strangers."

If this is a miracle baby, and God answered my parents' prayers, why can't we tell anyone?

I remained on constant guard, scared-stiff I would let our secret slip. It was okay when we talked with my grandparents about the baby, but I quickly caught on to keep my mouth shut around other people.

Maybe it was these scenarios that shaped me through life to display abnormal shyness. Always afraid I'd say the wrong thing.

+ + +

My mom's tummy inflated like a balloon.

"Mama, where are you going wearing one of Daddy's big shirts? You look funny."

"We have to go to court for Kevin's adoption. If the judge notices I'm pregnant, they'll take Kevin away from us."

Teardrops flowed. "Why w-w-would they do that? I thought he was ours. He's m-m-my brother. I don't want anyone to take h-h-h-h-him."

"His adoption isn't final yet. I'm sure it'll be okay. If I wear your Daddy's shirt, then the judge can't tell. Don't worry, Sweetheart."

Attempts to reassure me *not* to worry, forced me to worry even more. Tucked away in my little five-year-old mind brewed the horror that someone might snatch my brother.

I didn't care that we looked forward to the new miracle baby. I didn't want *him* yanked away from our family. I didn't want him replaced.

+ + +

We prepared for the baby's arrival.

The wooden crib transported from the attic, assembled a second time in our bedroom, once more scrubbed with pine-scented Lysol and polished with lemon Pledge.

Cloth diapers, with little blue bunnies printed on them, were washed with lots of bleach, hung on the clothesline, then meticulously folded and arranged neatly in our dresser drawer.

Lined up on top of the dresser, like my brother's toy soldiers, stood the baby powder, baby shampoo, Vaseline, alcohol, Q-tips, and my all-time-favorite, Johnson's Baby Lotion.

Glass baby bottles, with grossly huge brown rubber nipples, were sterilized in boiling water. Red-and-white cans of Carnation evaporated milk and clear bottles of sticky-sweet Karo syrup perched patiently upon the cupboard shelf and awaited the day to be stirred together and boiled into baby formula.

No doubt existed a baby would arrive, but—sshhhhhhh—we can't tell anyone just yet.

+ + +

My mom experienced migraine headaches. One rare night she disappeared to her bedroom. I tromped upstairs and knocked on her door.

"Come on in, Honey," she said.

"Are you okay, Mama?"

"Yes, I'm fine. Only another headache. Do you want to feel the baby move?"

The room is darkened, except one nightlight which glowed in the corner. She held the polka-dotted cloth ice pack on her forehead. I climbed onto her bed and laid down with my head on her outstretched arm. She gently positioned my right hand on her swollen tummy.

I felt movement, short sporadic thumps, up and down, like a kitten romping under a bedspread. This would be my baby brother or sister. My relationship with this sibling wouldn't be any different from the relationship with my brother.

Restless emotions still sprung up when I imagined anyone walking in and grabbing my brother. Except…the social worker had not visited for quite some time. Her absence helped calm my fears a tiny bit.

Dear God, please don't let anyone take this baby away from us.

My life existed as normal as any other child naturally born into a family. We celebrated family birthday parties, went on adventures to amusement parks and zoos, and visited lots of relatives. We loved each other. The perfect family.

The court finalized my brother's adoption in March 1960, which ended tension in the air. No further discussion of losing my brother. I guessed he was here to stay.

My sister, Sharon, entered our lives in June 1960. Her dazzling blue eyes, coal-black curly hair and chunky cheeks stole my heart. My miracle sister.

We adjusted to her entrance as smooth as my brother's. The one difference I observed—no visits from the social worker to check on this one. I don't know why.

Maybe the social worker approved of our perfect, little, clean house that one brisk October day and gave permission for my brother to stay.

But only time would tell.

Chapter 5

Lies

"Aren't you a cute little thing. You look just like your daddy."

My dad and I looked at each other. He winked. I smiled. We knew the truth. Peace surrounded me when I heard a comment that I looked like my Daddy. I'm confident. I'm part of the family. I didn't feel like an odd-ball merely because I'm adopted…not yet.

I'd lie awake at night. The full moon beamed through tree branches, casting shadows on our flowered wallpaper. Silhouettes appeared and morphed into faces. I molded shadows into whatever I wanted my birth mother to look like. Sometimes two faces appeared; one female, one male.

Why didn't she keep me? Did she think of me on my birthday? Is she married now?

I was nauseated every morning as I left for school. The nights before I'd scribble notes on torn scraps of paper. I deposited them in my nightstand drawer and hoped my mom would find them.

"Dear Mama: I love you so much. I don't want to go to school. I hate leaving you. It makes me sad. I want to stay with you all day. Love, Susan."

Burrowed into my bones is the fear I could come home one day and my brother or sister are gone, snatched from the jaws of our protective home, to live with another family.

+ + +

I began running away from school in second grade.

One requirement of Catholic school was attending Mass every morning. On the path from church to school, heads bowed and hands folded, when the single-file row of kids turned left towards the 100-year-old brick school, I marched straight ahead. And I didn't look back.

If I keep my head down and don't look over my

shoulder, the nuns won't see me. They won't run after me. They won't grab my shoulders and try shaking some sense into me.

I kept walking. I wanted to get home with my mom, brother and sister.

+ + +

After lunch one day in fourth grade, the nun in our class told me to go to the seventh grade classroom. Sister James Bernard wanted to see me.

Timidly I stepped into the room.

"Come here, young lady."

I cautiously took four steps and stopped.

"What do you think you were doing throwing this bologna sandwich in the garbage?"

"That's not mine, Sister."

"Speak up. I can't hear you."

"That's not mine. I had peanut butter and jelly today."

The half-eaten sandwich flapped within inches of my face.

"This *is* yours. I pulled it out of the garbage."

The veins in her forehead expanded and pulsed. Her face turned red.

"Do you know how wasteful this is? And you know it's a sin."

The soggy white bread opened its mouth and began spitting out the pink-brown, flat circle of compressed meat as Sister Bernard shook it closer to me.

Seconds before sprays of spit hit my face, I caught the stinging odor of pungent mustard.

"But it's n-n-not—"

"Don't lie to me, young lady. There are children starving in Africa. You committed a sin."

She knows I'm adopted. That's why she's picking on me. I'm not like the other kids. It's a sin to be born to a mother who isn't married. I'm being blamed for something I didn't do.

"Don't ever do this again. Do you hear me?"

"Yes, Sister."

She pitched the sandwich across the room into the gunmetal gray wastebasket beside her desk—and made two points.

She doesn't like me because I'm adopted. She knows I came from sin. I've heard a name they call people like this, a something child, but I can't remember what it is.

I'm not guilty of throwing away the sandwich. I'm not lying. It really wasn't mine. And I'm not guilty of sin just because I was adopted.

But by the time she finished screaming at me, I felt guilty of every sin ever invented.

In my mind I associated that everything bad happened to me because I was adopted. I pushed myself into feeling guilty of everything, whether I truly was or not.

+ + +

In fifth grade, friends asked, "Do you know who your *real* mother is? Have you ever tried looking for her?"

My first defensive attitude: *Of course I know my* real *mother, you idiot. She's home, doing laundry, ironing, cleaning, cooking, and always there when I need her.*

But the inner core of my soul cried: *I know* exactly *what mother you're talking about. I can't speak the words aloud. If I admit the truth, I'm a traitor to my parents. If my parents learn I'm a traitor, they'll be mad at me. I'll be in big trouble. And I don't want to hurt them.*

Locked-up questions grew behind prison bars in my mind. Nobody knew my scrambled imagination.

I need to release these questions. I need to flee this prison and verbalize my turmoil.

That's when insecurity took root.

Through grade school, I had the same friends. Our parents even went to school together. Living in a small town, my friends knew I was adopted, but never treated me different than anyone else. They accepted me into their groups.

But mentally I struggled like a stranger knocking to get in, quite the opposite of the questions inside my mind pounding to escape.

I'm the one who's adopted. None of my friends comprehended how my mind labored like a factory line, the same endless string of doubts parading in a circle like a merry-go-round. They couldn't perceive my false sense of security. If I attempted to explain my private battles, they still wouldn't be able to slip into my world where I silently floundered around with questions.

Always questions. Never answers.

My world sheltered a senseless void in my heart, an empty space where I tried developing into a whole person. But I carried the tag of "adoption."

+ + +

One day in sixth grade the nuns handed out green index cards with instructions to fill in our family information.

When I looked at the blank line labeled *Mother's Name*, I turned towards the girl sitting behind me and jokingly whispered, "I don't even know my real mother's name." We laughed.

But in a flash my mind forged ahead like a freight train. I swiftly looked around, to my left, then my right.

Did anyone else hear my remark? Why did I say that?

Breathing faster, I almost gasped. My heart pounded in my ears.

What if someone tells my parents what I said?

My hands shook.

It's the truth, though. That's what I was thinking.

Puking up lunch in front of classmates was not my intent, but the glob of peanut-butter-and-jelly sandwich blasted its way to my throat.

Swallow—take a deep breath—you can get out of this.

My stomach churned like a cement mixer.

I'm gonna be in so much trouble if my parents hear this.

My leg bounced.

I know what I'll do—what I always do to save myself.

After school I boldly tromped into the house, seized a warm, gooey chocolate chip cookie fresh off the cookie sheet, and shamelessly announced:

"Hi, Mama. Guess what? We filled out these cards in school today and it asked for mother's name. Barbara Ann Murphy said, 'You don't even know your real mother's name.'"

My mom's arm froze. She looked like one of those mannequins posed inside the window of J.C. Penney's. The harvest-gold towel, held midway between the white plastic laundry basket and the kitchen table, plopped down on top of multicolored towels.

In slow motion she turned her head and scowled, "What – did – you – say?"

"Barbara Ann Murphy said I don't even know my real mother's name."

I scrutinized her reaction.

I did it. She believes me. Now I won't get in trouble if they hear a different story from someone else.

The unforeseen unfolded.

She seized the shabby gray phone book, hurriedly ransacked through hundreds of pages, ravagingly ripping one page, narrowed her eyes enough to appear Oriental, and dialed the phone in disgust. She ensured each turn of the dial with her index finger pounded out her anger with a thunk.

"Mrs. Murphy, this is Mrs. Clum. Your daughter made a very nasty remark to my daughter today regarding her being adopted and not knowing her real mother. I AM HER MOTHER. And that's all there is to it. I'd appreciate you telling Barbara Ann to keep her mouth shut. This is not a subject we discuss. Keep your daughter away from Susan. I will not tolerate another remark like that."

SLAM!

My dumbfoundedness abruptly shifted to bewilderment. I focused on my white shoestrings, and took a shot at piecing together what just transpired.

Why did she get so nasty?

My eyes burned. The little plastic pieces on each end of the shoestrings moved, now blurred and swirled. Tears balanced on the edge of my lashes. If I blinked, they'd drip on my mom's fresh-waxed linoleum floor.

Turning her attention back to the clothes basket, she casually lifted the towel, without a hint she'd picked it up a second time. She folded it and steadily laid it on top of the other folded towels.

"Go do your homework now."

Relieved to be excused from the room, I aimlessly shuffled through the living room. But instead of my usual two-steps-at-a-time bouncing up the stairs, I gently placed one foot on a step at a time.

My mind whirled. My heart begged to cry out.

I was the guilty party for this incident. After all, I lied—a sinful habit developed later in life. I hadn't lied about not knowing my real mother's name, because it's the truth. But I lied to my mom.

Never again could I look Barbara Ann Murphy in the eyes. It was my fault she got in trouble. She knows I lied. I know I lied. I'm humiliated. I didn't *ever* want to talk to anyone *ever again* concerning my adoption.

Why won't Mama and Daddy let me talk about adoption and how I feel? If only...

I'm the one forced to exist in silence in my own miniature camouflaged world surrounded by mysteries and daydreams. I was the only person I could talk to in my mind dealing with these issues.

Even though I'm the special one and I'm the chosen one, I don't have the courage to approach my parents expecting answers. I'm the one drowning alone, isolated with my thoughts.

I don't want to be special anymore, because being special means I'm set apart from others. I don't want to be the only one in school who is adopted. Just fit in—that's all I wished.

I slipped into the belief that life as an adoptee or even mentioning adoption was disgraceful and naughty.

Chapter 6

The Question

A new adventure of boldness blossomed on my 13th birthday. My heart ached to ask my mom about my birth parents. Every time I contemplated the question, streams of sweat rippled from my armpits to my waist, my throat tightened, I couldn't swallow.

While I sat silent, friends bragged about their nationality. I'm never worthy enough to contribute to their verbal exchange, devoid of any clue what nationality I am.

Listening to stories of the country their grandparents immigrated from, how they resembled one relative or another, I sat silently on the sideline. Awkward moments for me. I suffered like an alien—although on the surface, I functioned in a normal world.

Maybe today I'll ask her.

Strolling downstairs, as I passed the white milk-glass vase filled with Lily of the Valley, the sweet floral smell caused me to sneeze. I tensely cleared my throat.

Within earshot, the WHAP-CLANK sounded like my mom hurled a fork into the kitchen sink. "Darn it! I burned the roast."

Not the right time.

Days passed. I laid awake each night and rephrased the question countless ways in my mind. The words must be perfect. My intent wasn't to upset my mom when I asked *the question*.

As I shuffled through the living room towards the den, I heard my mother's raised voice.

"What do you mean she took your Etch-A-Sketch, Sharon? Why did you let her? You go right back out there and get it back. Now!"

Okay. This wasn't the right time, either.

One day, while my mom braided my sister's hair, I blurted, "What did the adoption agency tell you about my biological parents?"

The Question

Sharon's blue eyes opened wide. Startled, she looked up at me with sparse brown freckles splashed across her cheeks. She wanted to vanish.

My neck grew hot. My face burned. My scalp tingled. I bit my tongue.

Mama held my sister's long black hair in both hands, the left braid halfway finished. She paused. I didn't know whether she'd answer honestly or become angry.

"All they told us was your mother was 17 and your father was 18, and they both had very high IQs. That's all we know," she curtly answered.

I squirmed. Well...I guess that's that!

She didn't appear angry. I didn't notice squinted eyes or an abrupt snap of her head to focus her glare at me.

But I learned from her straighter, taller-than-normal posture, the nose-in-the-air attitude and the pursed-lipped facial expression implied anymore questions would be a crappy idea.

My fingers skimmed along the arm of the black bench when I turned and walked away.

Chapter 7

The Move

Eighth grade graduation was not the only momentous milestone that happened in my life during 1968.

Three months before the end of the school year my mother announced, "Your daddy got a new job in Ohio. We'll be moving in August. But you can't say a word. If anyone asks you what's going on, just tell them you don't know anything."

More secrets. More lies.

How can I face my friends, knowing I'm forced to leave them, and not share our family secret?

With no one to talk to concerning my emotions, once again I tied a knot around this bag of secrets, vibrations of insecurity, and kept these mysteries hidden in the pit of my stomach.

I lived in Monroe, Michigan, my entire life of 13 years—if you don't count the three weeks before my adoption that I didn't yet know of my whereabouts. In August we would move to Van Wert, Ohio, a smaller town than Monroe, in the middle of wheat and corn fields.

The possibility crossed my mind that maybe we were moving to get farther away from my birth mother.

Before we packed up and left, I searched for clues:

Instead of praying with my head bowed in church, I opened my eyes, raised them just enough to look around, spied on people to see if another woman looked at me—then I'd know she was my birth mother.

Standing around the corner of our kitchen, I eavesdropped when my mom talked on the phone—a whispered voice served as a sign she's talking to my birth mother.

Riding in the car, if my mom slowed down as we passed a woman on the sidewalk, I promptly noted her physical features, because if she was short, with dark hair and dark eyes like me, and if she even slightly appeared like she was gifted with a high IQ, then she's definitely my birth mother.

On one hand, the anticipated move to Ohio invited excitement. We would live in a brand new house with new wallpaper on my bedroom walls. We'd attend a new church, instead of the 134-year-old Catholic church in Monroe. We would shop in new stores. We would have more than one bathroom.

But on the other hand, I grew more apprehensive. In Monroe, for eight years I enjoyed the same school friends. Now we'd be moving 115 miles away to a small town with one public high school, where I knew no one.

Even though in a small town you knew everyone and everyone knew you, I always considered myself inferior. I counted my blessings if someone asked for my friendship. I never allowed myself the pleasurable satisfaction to feel worthy enough to be accepted as anyone's friend, although I had a couple close friends, and still cherish their friendships to this day.

But inside I withdrew as the lone adopted person. I'm still the only one adopted—the special one. In my mind, I set myself apart with the tag of "adoption."

As we pulled out of Monroe one last time, I watched the scenery whiz by.

We passed the Monroe Rod and Gun Club where my Papa took me for yearly Easter egg hunts, amidst shotguns and fishing poles.

Crossing over the River Raisin, a dead fish smell lingered around the statue of General Custer.

Rolling past the A&W drive-in, the thought of their famous ice-cold root beer made my mouth water.

The biting smell spewing from the cast-iron steel factory stung my nose and I choked. I pressed my hand against the tan leather seat as my stomach convulsed from car sickness.

I treasured the only hometown I'd known. We now approached the unknown.

+ + +

Timid and terrified—that's how I entered the first day of my freshman year. I wanted to throw up. I wanted to run and hide.

I assumed everyone in public high school would be nice, like enforced by the nuns in Catholic grade school. I wasn't familiar with cliques, bad crowds or good crowds. Through high school, I oftentimes became involved with the bad crowd. I didn't understand you shouldn't do this in a public high school. You can't be friends with every person.

My teenage years were rocky. I tried filling the dark cave in my heart, tried to find myself, tried to fit in with my peers, as I floundered in the hallway among the sea of students searching for acceptance, approval, recognition.

I didn't recognize this behavior existed among teenagers. I believed my insecurity of worthlessness continued because I'm adopted.

If only my parents would have allowed me to talk about adoption, I wouldn't be forced to keep my questions secret. If only I knew someone else adopted, I'd have a person to connect with or talk to about my jumbled confusion. If only…

+ + +

I never dismissed the possibility we moved to get farther away from my birth mother. I didn't know where she lived, but maybe my parents knew. It seemed odd that I asked my mom a question regarding my adoption, then shortly thereafter she announced we'd be moving.

Through the years, the anticipation of

someday finding her crossed my mind—but that's all—nothing but fleeting thoughts. Ideas that couldn't be watered like flower seeds and bloom into life. Notions that must stay restrained in my mind. Doubts that shall never cross my lips. Never spoken to anyone.

I hesitated to romp around in my head and invent images of my birth family for fear my mom could read my mind. I hoped someday my parents would be able to talk about adoption.

Through high school I never met an adoptee. Strange, isn't it? Perhaps someone lived in town who had been adopted; but maybe, like my family, they weren't allowed to mention it.

We only spoke of being special and chosen—but never adoption. If someone else initiated the subject, it seemed acceptable to talk about it. But if I brought up the subject, my mother glared at me with her infamous evil eye.

In biology class we studied heredity and genes. If someone had brown eyes, then one parent might have blue and the other brown, or both parents have brown eyes. Brown hair most of the time resulted from both parents with brown or black hair.

I tucked away these crucial facts in my

memory. I may need this information later. I might be able to narrow down what my birth parents look like, right?

+ + +

As a youngster, my adoption never created conflict with my parents. I never discerned anything wrong with me. Happy and content with my family, I couldn't have been blessed with any better parents.

But as I grew older, the questions grew louder. They multiplied and expanded. Occurred more frequent. I developed a dominating curiosity.

On the outside I appeared normal. But the adoption war raged in the battlefield of my mind. I backed away from reality with a sense of insanity.

Low self-esteem.
Insecurity.
Worthlessness.

Chapter 8

Toes

With every passing year, I dedicated additional time reflecting on my birth parents.

Church on Sunday became more of a daydreaming appointment between me and God. I pleaded with Him to reveal answers. My mind wandered instead of praying. Although I had faith and trusted in God, no cloud of answers burst through the stained glass windows.

Reaching for any answer, I fixed my eyes on the corn field next to our house, and my questions twisted into bizarreness at times.

What if she lived on the other side of this corn field? Maybe we moved here to torment her— she would be able to see me, but couldn't touch.

The Special Chosen One

What if she's dead and buried in that corn field? Do I dare wander around at night searching for a grave?

What if she's one of my teachers at school? Which one had dark hair, dark eyes and was 17 years older than me? Mrs. Jaffrey? No. Mrs. Landry? No.

Wait—what if we moved here because my birth father lived here? Maybe he's one of my teachers. Let's see…there's Mr. Wall. He's short, dark hair, dark eyes. Daddy golfed with him. No—can't be him. He's too old.

+ + +

My second cousin, Bobby, often popped into my head.

A Marine—that's Bobby. I idolized his sincere smile, warm-hearted jokes, genuine laugh and jet black hair. He's fun. He always wrapped his arms around me resulting in tight hugs.

More than once he stated, "You know, you're my favorite. Look, I carry your picture with me all the time and show it to everyone."

To prove it, he unfolded his wallet. The first picture displayed was me as a toddler. I loved his visits.

+ + +

From time to time my mom observed, "You have toes like your grandmother's."

I knew she referred to my adoptive grandmother. But puzzled why she'd make that kind of statement. Both of us knew I was adopted. No way had I genetically inherited my grandmother's toes.

These comments controlled my mind for days, but then I'd dismiss the notion. I wouldn't rock the boat by asking for explanations. I am the one who wouldn't hurt them or disrupt our love.

After all, I was chosen. I'm special. I wouldn't demolish our calm, peaceful family. I kept the questions confined.

Instead, I convinced myself that my mature teenage mind was capable of adding two and two together on my own.

+ + +

Some Saturdays when Daddy was golfing and Mama out of town shopping, there was plenty of time to be sneaky. I gathered the photo albums. Quickly turning the plastic-covered pages, I searched only for photos of Bobby.

There's one. He's in his military uniform. Look at his dark eyebrows. I'd gaze at my eyebrows. Yep, mine looked the same as his.

Another one of him and Aunt Margaret. He's smiling really big. I leaped from my bedroom floor, squinted at the mirror attached to the antique-yellow dresser and smiled really big, trying to make my smile identical to his. Yep, I have his smile, too.

Here's one where he held a bottle of beer. Look at his nose. It's big. I dashed into the bathroom, knocking over the green bottle of Prell shampoo my sister left on the floor. I flipped the light switch and studied my nose reflected in the oval gold-rimmed mirror above double sinks. I ran back to the brown photo album, analyzed his nose again.

Wait! John has a big nose, Aunt Margaret, Aunt Mary, Uncle Steve, my Daddy. Everyone in the family had a big nose. They are Hungarian. They all had big noses. Oh, my gosh…I must be Hungarian.

Bobby is my birth father.

I struggled in an effort to arrange the

theories as fast as they popped into my head.

> Bobby was 18 years older than me.
> My birth father was 18 years older than me.
>
> I had toes like my grandmother.
> I must have gotten this genetic trait from that side of my family, and from Bobby.
>
> Bobby's short.
> I'm short.
>
> Bobby had dark skin.
> I had olive-colored skin.
>
> Bobby, dark hair and dark eyes.
> Me—dark hair and dark eyes.

That's why we never talked about my adoption. He's my father. They kept my adoption within the family. I'd read about those secrets in other families. That's the reason I'm his favorite and he carried my picture in his wallet and he's always happy to see me.

> I'm positive he's my birth father.
>
> Or was he?
>
> I wondered what his toes looked like.

Chapter 9

Does Anyone Know?

What's wrong with me? My mind spun like a record. Something must be wrong if I wanted to search for my birth mother.

I never intended to hurt my parents. That's the last thing I wanted. I simply itched to know my background, my nationality and who I looked like. I cried myself to sleep.

Nothing more was mentioned after the guidance counselor informed my mom I wanted to find my birth mother. Nothing about how I must be crazy.

I talked about selective subjects. I tiptoed on egg shells. I wouldn't rock the boat. I tossed my search dream on the back burner. I noticed my parents' anguish, although I didn't understand, even after I described my feelings.

I moved on with our normal, happy lifestyle. Actually, our family life could be portrayed as the *Leave It to Beaver* family. Everything always organized in our house, laundry, ironing, dinner every night at 5:30, and breakfast each morning before school.

Our family was affectionate. We thrived on love. We lived the dream, the typical American family. I didn't have any reason to leave my family or replace them.

But the nagging, empty gap in my heart lingered. And I remained silent.

I continued piano lessons, attended school, played in the band, joined the church youth group, rejoiced at high school football games, and enjoyed sleepovers with friends.

But as time went on, the craving to find my birth mother wormed its way toward the front of my mind. The yearning increased.

The voice I heard rumbled. A tugging urgency to find her—uncover the truth to my adoption.

At the stubborn age of 16, I started the

search, and never told my adoptive parents. I talked to a couple friends. I devised different methods, various options, with the ultimate goal that my parents not find out.

The first option: Publish a personal ad in the newspaper. I figured with my first and middle name, along with my birthdate, at least one person knew something. My birth mother had parents, probably brothers or sisters, friends, or other relatives who might talk. *One* person in Jackson, Michigan, existed who could answer my questions.

The main problem: How to instruct someone to answer the ad. I couldn't give my home address or phone number. No computers or cell phones in the 1970s. One girlfriend offered to let me use her address as a point of contact. Sounded simple enough. I learned the cost of the ad and used my babysitting money to pay for it. I placed the ad in the Jackson newspaper where I was born. I will get an answer. My spirit soared with anticipation of finally finding out about *me*.

The ad read:

"Anyone knowing of a Susan Marie born on July 18, 1954, in Jackson, Michigan, please contact..."

I pestered my friend day after day, week after week. I never received one response. My spirit crumbled. Perhaps a relative read my ad, and maybe my mom was mentally handicapped, but they were afraid to tell me.

Maybe even my birth mother saw it, but didn't want anything to do with me. Am I the result of a rape?

Is she a rich and famous person and can't be exposed?

Numerous scenarios rushed through my mind as I concocted excuses why I hadn't heard from anyone yet.

Even though I didn't receive any answers, I'm comforted I didn't hurt my parents. I executed this plan so secretly, my parents never suspected…or so I thought.

I scooped the Ruffles potato chip through the onion dip. One bite and my mother asked, "Did you ever get an answer to the ad you put in the Jackson newspaper?"

The chip in my mouth turned limp and soggy. I couldn't swallow.

I shivered. My body froze. Heart paralyzed. Queasy stomach.

"How did you know about that?"

"I'm not going to tell you, but I have my ways."

To this day I have not solved the mystery surrounding how she knew. She never told me. I sensed somebody, somewhere, knew more about *me* than I did.

The questions stayed secure inside my heart, like a safe-deposit box, except no one held the key.

+ + +

Another time my parents didn't approve of a boyfriend I liked. They wanted me to end the relationship.

"Do you want to end up like your mother?"

My mother? Mama was pregnant before they got married? She's my birth mother?

They swiftly deciphered the expression of puzzlement on my face.

My dad corrected himself. "No, your real mother. Do you want to end up like her? Don't you think you owe us something?"

What did I owe them?

"No."

"What? You don't think you owe us anything for all the years we have taken care of you?"

I didn't comprehend what he was talking about. My sense of reason twisted out of focus.

Is this a requirement of an adopted child? To owe something to the parents who took them in and raised them?

Why wasn't I told about this? I'm baffled.

I created an evil darkness—hurt my adoptive parents. I explained my distress. I didn't want to replace them. *They* were my parents. But they never understood and refused to see my viewpoint. I intuitively sensed, once again, the emotional anguish that questions were not permitted nor tolerated.

What had I done? Why am I so cruel and insensitive to their emotions? Was I unappreciative? Did I only care about *my* desires to search—find some link to my past?

At the moment I abandoned the entire idea. I consoled myself with the fact that when I'm older and eventually left home, I would resume this passion. My adoptive parents wouldn't know then.

A postponement lessened any further chance to hurt them.

As an adoptee, I never experienced completeness. An empty, unfilled hole simmered deep within my soul. I wasn't a whole person, with no sense of a real connection to anyone. The unspoken belief was that my concept of disassociation was not *normal*.

Something is terribly wrong with me. How dare I reject my adoptive parents by even thinking about anyone else other than the family who raised me.

The more I tried deciphering why I felt this way, the more irrational I became. There's no reason for me to harbor these feelings. I experienced a happy childhood, stable environment, fantastic, loving parents, and a brother and sister whom I grew up with.

My prayer: That she would find me first. Then I wouldn't be blamed. Then my self-imposed guilt of searching would be lifted off my shoulders.

Chapter 10

Cheeseburger & Fries Confession

What if I fell in love not knowing he's my brother? Or he also was adopted, didn't know it, and after marriage discovered we were cousins?

Fear of the unknown hung like an icicle on a warm day, dripping one sluggish drop after another, waiting to fall, but not knowing when the collapse would take place. Bizarre images flashed in my head, lingered only a second, replaced by another freakish suspicion.

+ + +

I fell in love with my sweetheart two months before high school graduation. After we dated a few months, I decided to tell him I'm adopted. I procrastinated. I dreaded sharing this information with the fear I might be abandoned.

Who wanted me if I didn't know my nationality? What if his parents rejected me because I didn't know what genes I had? They don't know what kind of grandchildren I would be able to give them.

I replayed the confession in my mind and rephrased it every which way.

We sat across from each other in Burger Chef, eating our cheeseburgers and fries. Ignoring my unsettled stomach, I built up the courage to tell him.

"I have something to tell you about myself. I'm adopted. I don't know who my birth parents are."

"Okay. So?"

"I hope this doesn't affect our relationship."

"It's no big deal."

Really? That simple? I'm surprised he accepted the news so quick. I breathed a sigh of relief. I rested easier now. He knew my *secret*.

We married a year later. I wish I could tell you my adoption didn't affect our marriage. But I can't.

Periodically I revealed ideas to my husband regarding my search, which usually ended in an argument. He supported the same opinion as my parents. Even though he said it was no big deal, he didn't understand.

"Why would you want to do that? Your parents are your parents. I don't think it's a good idea. I'm not in favor of it."

Nobody understood! And frequently even I didn't understand.

I wandered around reflecting more on finding my birth mother. I couldn't grasp an understanding of why I suffered this fixation. I was desperate and distraught with my obsession.

I lived isolated in my solitary world of adoption. No one to talk to—not even my own husband. He wasn't on my side. I'm abandoned. Lonely. Rejected.

My husband knew where *he* came from, *his* time of birth, *his* birth weight, and *his* nationality. If he ever had questions about *his* background, he could always approach his parents, ask them, explain *his* desire to learn his roots and heredity, and nobody would challenge *his* motives, nor would there be anything wrong with *him*!

If it was no big deal before we married, why

can't it be no big deal now if I want to search? Did he mean it at the time? Or had he lied to me?

Who was *I*, Susan Marie, supposed to go to when I had the same questions? Who was *I* supposed to go to when I longed to catch a glimpse of anyone who looked like me? Or when doctors asked about *my* medical background?

I did not know.

Lord, I'm emotionally exhausted. Why can't You perform a miracle so this insane turmoil will end?

Chapter 11

I Don't Know

Five months of wedded bliss. Greg served in the Air Force. I babysat.

Growing up, I dreamed of raising many children. Don't all little girls dream of the day they get married and start a family? But my vision of becoming a mommy mushroomed into obsession.

Family and friends cautioned me, "You're too young." "Wait until you're older." "Wait until you've been married longer." "Wait until you're financially stable."

Wait. Wait. Wait.

I can't wait. I don't want to wait. I wanted a baby—and I wanted one now.

Any woman on the path to fulfill her nurturing instinct becomes consumed with expectations of pregnancy. But I ended up overboard, way out there—beyond control, as my husband would say. I submerged myself with plans, more so than the average female—that is, the average female who is not adopted.

Later in life, I realized I subconsciously reached out, desperate to seize any concrete form of existence. Motivated to discover a connection to something, anything or anyone, I prayed for a miracle. I knew God, but at this point in my life I didn't walk with Him or trust Him for the results I desired.

Nine months after our wedding, I'm pregnant and 20 years old. We would now be able to share our love with a child and thrilled with the future anticipation as parents.

+ + +

On my first visit to the obstetrician, I filled out basic paperwork. In the Family Medical History section, I hesitated. Between my index finger and thumb, I twirled a section of hair. I needed to think for a minute. The words blurred on the paper.

My mom always completed the paperwork for doctors when I lived at home. She filled in that section with their own medical information and pretended I came from them.

But I'm *adopted* and this one-word tidbit of crucial information never entered my medical records. In their eyes, I'm their child. I didn't have any background history before being placed in their arms. My parents convinced themselves that I inherited their own family history when they adopted me.

Not comprehending this as a child, I never questioned.

I now realized I lived a lie.

Blinking my eyes, I forced myself back to reality. I ignored teardrops smudging my handwriting. Flickering images of my birth mother fluttered through my mind.

It doesn't matter, I told myself. I'm only having a baby. What does the medical history of my birth parents have to do with anything? I knew nothing anyway. Can't be a big deal.

I contemplated my options. I'm now on my own, married and pregnant. I could do what I wanted and make decisions by myself.

Do I continue to live a lie and write the medical information of my adoptive parents? Or do

I begin to announce the truth?

For the first time in my life, I gathered the fortitude to write ADOPTED.

I winced.

The nurse and the obstetrician glanced over my file and ensured everything was in order. I observed facial expressions when they reached the ADOPTED section. I anticipated a reaction. But they didn't appear surprised.

They didn't ask questions. I'm right. No big deal.

Throughout my pregnancy, I read many books, learned about the growth and development of babies before birth. Laying my hands on my swollen stomach, I felt rippling movement.

A foot? A hand?

It didn't matter. This baby is a miracle.

Lounging in my comfy green rocking chair, I rejoiced in amazement at the growth of the baby inside of me. I laid my head back and closed my eyes.

Did my mother do the same when she was

pregnant with me? Had she paid attention to my movements as I grew in her tummy?

+ + +

The first six months of pregnancy were normal.

One day in July the expected aches and pains of pregnancy progressed into a fever, back pain and endless vomiting. Friends advised, "Being pregnant isn't always fun. There will be times when you don't feel well. You're gonna have a lot of odd feelings going on."

What I experienced must be normal then.

Lethargic, I laid on the couch three days. My fever spiked higher, with delirious chills and shakes. Even small sips of water spewed out of my mouth. My husband called the doctor and immediately rushed me to the hospital.

I wasn't concerned. After all, I'm pregnant. This is normal.

Metal doors swung open and closed as people in blue scrubs and white coats scurried in and out. Syringes drew blood. Catheters collected urine. Large-bore needles were shoved into the veins of both arms. Three bags of clear liquid dangled on silver posts above my head. Every

10 minutes, in the midst of commotion, I hugged a way-too-small plastic bowl.

I'm young and naive. I didn't comprehend all the fuss.

After medical tests, the diagnosis: An acute kidney infection. I assumed the doctor would get rid of the infection and everything would be fine.

Interns wheeled me into an isolation room. Every 15 minutes, nurses flung back the bedsheets, slapped cold stethoscopes on my stomach and tried locating the baby's heartbeat.

Never before had a doctor asked specific questions that involved my medical background.

"How was your mother's pregnancy?"

"I don't know."

"What was her medical background?"

"I don't know."

"Were there any complications with your birth?"

"I...don't...know," I whispered.

A nagging voice nudged me to search for my birth mother.

Did she have problems with her pregnancy? Maybe she developed a kidney infection with me and that's why I have one now.

Lying in a hospital bed, alone, in the bare, cold room, my thoughts drifted. The baby squirmed around.

Had my mom been happy when pregnant with me?

I pictured delivering our baby and then giving it away. I couldn't do that. I questioned how my mother felt after having me.

Did she hold me or even look at me?

Why did she give me up for adoption?

Why?

After two weeks on IV antibiotics and in isolation, I recovered enough to return home.

When the nurse prepared my discharge

papers, she asked, "Did your mother have any complications during her pregnancy or your birth?"

With tears in my eyes, "I don't know."

Chapter 12

I'm Not Interested

⌢⌣

The last two months of pregnancy we prepared for the birth of our first baby. In 1974, routine ultrasounds were not performed to detect a baby's sex. So we did what everyone else did in those days, chose common baby colors appropriate for either sex: green, yellow, white and lilac.

Sleepers and blankets agitated inside the washing machine with Ivory Snow laundry detergent and rinsed in Downy fabric softener.

The identical cloth diapers flaunted by my brother, sister and me, with the little blue bunnies printed on them, were sanitized with bleach and hung from the clothesline, exactly like I remembered my mom doing when my brother and sister joined the family.

Sitting on our red plaid couch, rays of sunlight cut through the cloudy trailer window onto the ugly fire-engine red carpet. I meticulously folded each piece of baby clothing. Thoughts of my birth mom leisurely strolled into my mind.

Did she do this for me before I was born? Had she planned to keep me?

Maybe someday the questions would be answered.

+ + +

Amy was born in October 1974, a healthy 7-pound 2-ounce baby girl. She displayed a headful of black hair, dark eyes, and olive-colored skin.

After her birth, my doctor announced, "Well, despite all the problems with your kidneys during the pregnancy, your baby is healthy."

"What do you mean?"

"Kidney infections increase the risk of premature birth, developmental delays, and sometimes even death, for the baby or the mother."

I remained speechless.

"Did your mother have any problems throughout her pregnancy with you?"

"I don't know."

"Were there any complications with your birth?"

"I don't know. I'm adopted."

What dark secrets laid buried in my family's medical background?

+ + +

I experienced a powerful bond with my daughter, staring at her for hours. We cuddled. I buried my nose in the folds of her neck to smell Johnson's baby lotion. I sniffed her hair. I studied her facial features, her fingers and…her toes.

Her toes!

Did they look like mine?

Why am I mesmerized with her? I clearly realized she's the *first* blood relative with whom I felt connected.

Reality dawned.

She really *was* my first blood relative I came

face to face with in my entire life. I'd never even seen one picture of anyone related to me.

Here we go again. The impulse to search for my birth mother cropped up. I'm lost. Confused.

Not aware of how or where to begin. We lived 10 hours away from my birthplace. We didn't have money for a search, besides the fact I didn't know what a search involved.

Instead, I scrunched those emotions tightly together, tied them up and crammed them into the depths of my heart. I assumed my role as a mother.

+ + +

At age 22, our second child was on the way. I visited a different obstetrician this time. But he asked the same questions.

"What is your family's medical background?"

"I don't know."

"How was your mother's pregnancy with you?"

"I don't know."

"What was your birth weight?"

"I don't know."

"Were there any complications with your birth?"

"I...don't...know."

Experiencing slight back pain and low-grade fever at five months of pregnancy, I recognized symptoms of a kidney infection. I was hospitalized a few days, given IV antibiotics, quickly recovered and discharged. Thank God, we'd caught it early enough this time.

I remember the day my doctor invited me into his office and closed the door.

"I can find your birth mother for you, if you want me to."

Grinding my teeth, I held my breath and deliberated. I stared past the doctor, through the window behind him.

Gloomy and gray the middle of January in the Upper Peninsula of Michigan. Fluffy shimmering snowflakes created random patterns in the air. The room twirled. I'm woozy.

The doctor sat serenely poised behind the

desk in his squeaky leather chair while I sat silent across from him.

Exhaling, I murmured, "No, that won't be necessary. I'm not interested."

Wait!

What was I saying?

Why the disorder in my mind? What compelled me to refuse his offer?

I straddled the fence: Did I want to find my birth parents at the risk of losing my adoptive parents?

I feared my adoptive parents may find out I'm searching again. I didn't want to sadden or disappoint them. Later in life, I often regretted not accepting his offer.

+ + +

I replayed the scene in my mind, like a phonograph needle skipping across a black vinyl record:

I can find your birth mother . . . if you want . . .

No, that won't be . . . I'm not interested . . .

I can find her. . . I can find her . . . if you want . . .

No . . . no . . . not interested . . .

Driving home from Ishpeming to Sands, I heard fragments of a news report from the local radio station 92.3.

". . . song Convoy hits number one on the charts . . . George Bush becomes 11th director of CIA . . . NBC replaces peacock logo . . . sentenced to life for attempting to shoot President Ford . . ."

Wendy, our second daughter, was born in April 1976, at 5 pounds 11 ounces and healthy, with black hair and blue eyes.

Blue eyes?

I understood all babies are born with blue eyes. But after a few months her eyes stayed blue. Greg's eyes were green, Amy's dark brown and mine brown. No one on Greg's side of the family had blue eyes.

And I only imagined what my mother-in-law thought.

Creeping up again—like the peanut-butter-and-jelly sandwich in grade school—the anguished urge to search. I knew the blue eyes were inherited from someone on *my* side of the family.

Chapter 13

The Brown Metal Box

On my 24th birthday I knew in my heart the moment to start and finish my search is now. Time slipped by. I am defeated. I'd never meet my birth mother, gaze into her eyes, hear her voice or catch the scent of her perfume.

Knowing her age at the time of my birth and her high IQ wasn't enough to satisfy me any longer. I needed to know more—more about me.

I surrendered to the fact I wouldn't be able to do this on my own. I needed help and wanted to talk with someone else who's an adoptee.

After weeks of seeking a search and support group in Toledo, Ohio, where we lived at the time, I discovered ALMA (Adoptees' Liberty Movement Association).

When I stepped into my first meeting, detecting the aroma of fresh-brewed coffee, my jaw hung open at the roomful of people. I focused upon the speakers—adoptees and birth parents searching and reunited, and amazing adoptive parents in support of their adopted child searching—as they spoke in public of their secrets.

Most of their terminology I didn't understand: Sealed records, original birth certificate, Decree of Adoption, release of confidentiality, nonidentifying information, and search registries.

After the meeting I introduced myself to the group leader, Cheryl, an adoptee reunited with her birth family. We arranged to meet at her house the next week.

+ + +

"I'm so happy to meet another adopted person," I said. "I don't know where to begin."

"Do you have possession of your original birth certificate?"

"Yeah. My mom gave me my birth certificate when I got married."

"What are the parents' names listed?"

"Well...m-m-my parents...my adoptive parents."

"Susan, that's your amended birth certificate; the one issued after adoption, incorporating your adopted name."

"That's the only birth certificate I have. I was told all adoption records were permanently sealed forever, and nobody had access to anything."

"You need to acquire your original birth certificate filed with the State which will verify your original birth name and the names of your birth parents. That certificate isn't sealed."

"What? I have another birth certificate? I had a different name before I was adopted?"

I chomped faster on my Wrigley's spearmint gum.

"Yes. Every person is named at birth and issued an original birth certificate. When a child is adopted, the adoptive parents assign a new name and an amended birth certificate is filed with the State Department of Vital Statistics. The adoptive parents are presented with a Decree of Adoption listing the child's original name so if the birth mother shows up at the door and says she—"

I couldn't concentrate as Cheryl finished her sentence. I scratched at the candy-apple red cover of my notebook.

"Well, how do I get my original birth certificate and Decree of Adoption?"

"You can ask your adoptive parents for the—"

"Oh, no, that's out of the question. No way can I ask them for anything. They never want to talk about it. So, I guess there's no way I can find out."

My eyes filled with tears. My hope squashed.

"That's incorrect. Many methods are used to gather data. Once you obtain your original name, you can request your original birth certificate using that name. The certificate will show at least your birth mother's name and sometimes the birth father."

Cheryl outlined instructions to request nonidentifying information from the adoption agency or courthouse who finalized the adoption.

"This could reveal where your birth mother lived, her religion, education, medical history, or any siblings. You should also request the Decree of

Adoption with the off-chance an office worker might send it to you by mistake."

+ + +

Indirectly, I tried unearthing little clips of information from my adoptive mother. I backslid to my familiar pattern of lying to gather facts about myself that *normal* people take for granted.

I leaned on the green plastic kitchen chair, sticky with maple syrup from pancakes we ate for breakfast, and held myself upright. I dialed my parents' number.

Clearing my throat several times, I struggled to sound calm, while droplets of sweat oozed into wet circles under the arms of my T-shirt. I swiftly fabricated a story in my mind.

After the mundane "How are you? How's your weather?" I shifted the conversation towards my original motive for calling my mom.

"A friend of ours recently adopted a baby. The court gave them some kind of paper, I think an Adoption Decree or something like that. It gives the original name of their baby and also shows the birth mother's name. They were upset because they really didn't want to know."

Standing on tip-toes, I locked my jaw,

squeezed my eyes shut in a grimace, and squirmed while waiting for my mom's response.

"Oh, Honey, we never got anything like that when we got you."

It worked. She believed my story. I perfected the disgusting art of lying.

"We went through Catholic Charities. My friend, Mrs. Burroughs, worked there. All they told us was your name was Susan Marie. We liked the name, so we kept it. But we never got any kind of papers. I'm glad we didn't. I wouldn't want to know any names, either. You belong to us and nobody else."

Ah-ha. My original name, Susan Marie? Hmmmm….that's news to me! My birth mother named me Susan Marie, which stuck to me like glue after adoption. Now I embraced a small tidbit of fresh information.

I'd lie awake at night trying to devise a way to sneak my adoption records out of the courthouse.

If I hid in the bathroom until they closed, I'd have the entire building to myself for the night. Would it be against the law trying to find information regarding my own self?

But if I got caught, I wonder how long I'd have to stay in jail. I made a mental note to check out that law the next time I visited the library.

+ + +

Suspicious that my parents didn't receive a Decree of Adoption, I ached to dig further. Christmas approached. I devised a plan.

"Greg, I know where my parents keep their metal box with all the adoption papers. After dinner when everyone goes to the family room, I'm gonna get the box, sneak into the bathroom and try to find something more. You need to distract them and keep them in there."

While the flavor of sweet apple pie lingered on my lips, the time arrived to execute my plan.

Grab and run.

Quick. Quick. Quick.

Don't let the red plastic handle fall or it will clink on top of the faded brown metal box.

Find the folder labeled Susan's Adoption printed in blue ink. Flip through the papers. Skim for unfamiliar names.

Mrs. Burroughs…I already knew her name.

Hurry. Hurry. Hurry.

Catholic Charities…knew that one.

Time ticked away with each heartbeat.

Monroe County Courthouse…knew that one, too.

Nothing. Absolutely nothing new.

Voices. Getting louder.

Arrange the papers in the same orderly fashion inside the dog-eared vanilla-colored file folder. Don't let the lock click too loud when I pinch the metal tab into the opening.

Footsteps in the hallway, passing the bathroom door, faded into a distant bedroom.

My hand stopped in midair as I reached for the shiny gold lock in the center of the doorknob. I sucked in a breath. The woodsy pine candle scent tickled my nose. I stifled a sneeze. I looked at the yellow-gold shag carpet.

How can I get out of here? I didn't know if anyone wandered away from the family room while I hid. Oh, crap…I hadn't envisioned a bad ending to my scheme.

I'd get caught with the cold metal box in my hand, forced to concoct a lie. But what kind of lie would explain leaving the bathroom clutching the box that contained nothing but adoption papers?

Shaking my head at my stupidity, I pressed my ear against the door and listened for noise. I exhaled and gulped in another deep breath, unlocked the door, opened it, and peeked around the corner to the right and left.

Run. Get the box back in the closet before you get caught.

I did it!

Now I was about to dart back into the bathroom and throw up my mom's Christmas dinner.

Chapter 14

Tear-Stained Letter

The complex battle encountered throughout the next few months boggled my mind. I needed to find my original last name.

Beginning in Jackson, Michigan, where I was born, I mailed letters to every doctor, hospital, elementary school, high school, church, unwed mothers' home, adoption agency, library, and genealogical society.

I typed each one on white bond paper, with carbon and tissue-paper thin onionskin, rolled into a black, manual Smith-Corona typewriter. All 137 letters read the same:

> *"Could you please tell me if you have any records at all for a baby girl, Susan Marie, born*

> *July 18, 1954, in Jackson, Michigan, to a 17-year-old girl."*

One by one, responses found their way to my mailbox. Most replied:

> *"We do not have any record of a Susan Marie born on that date."*

A few informed me:

> *"You need to supply us with a last name in order to search our records further."*

I hissed, "That's what I'm trying to find out, you dummy, my last name," and flapped the paper as if swatting at a swarm of bees.

My husband knew I was enraged and what type of response I received.

+ + +

As a child, I shuffled around the 75-foot perimeter of the touristy Blue Hole in Sandusky, Ohio, claimed to be a bottomless pool of blue water. I was terrified believing the water went down and down forever and ever.

But now I felt like the Blue Hole, with a bottomless stomach and a heart diving in an endless spiral, around and down.

+ + +

Sometime during the search, my husband softened and became more supportive. He recognized the emotional pain, physical stress and mental chaos raging inside: weeping, not pacified with his arms wrapped around me; fatigue from sleepless nights; frequent outbursts and stuttering nonsense when I invented absurd scenarios. He honored the seriousness of uncovering information about myself.

We attended church more regularly now. My search for a more meaningful relationship with Jesus expanded on a daily basis. I begged and pleaded, and learned the only One who could ever help me was God. I invested complete faith and trust in His power.

On Saturday, October 21, 1978, I experienced a spiritual eye-opener. While in church service, I prayed for myself, as usual, distraught, and craving God's intervention to find my birth mother. In the middle of service, a voice behind me faintly whispered, "You will find her."

I spun around. An empty pew! My mind played games. I panicked and couldn't suck in enough air to breathe. Was I insane?

Once again I clearly heard, "You will find her." A second time I reeled around. No one! A warm blanket washed over my body and an awareness of peace resided inside. I believed I would find my birth mother. I sensed the time was near. I trusted God.

Little did I know He'd work so quick—after all, only three months elapsed since I started my full-time search.

Ten days later, on Tuesday, October 31, 1978, I entered our living room after work. My husband stood with his hands behind his back. "Would it make you happy to know where you were born?"

"Greg, I know where I was born. In Jackson, Michigan."

"No. I mean…if you really knew *where* you were born."

Annoyed, not in any mood for jokes, I winced as an electrical shock sparked in my head, as if a demon flipped a pain switch. Unable to focus, I tried to pray away the compressed, nauseating knot in my stomach.

He extended his hand and presented an envelope, with a smile on his face. The return address indicated an unwed mother's home in Jackson, Michigan, the Florence Crittenton Home, 1603 Lansing Avenue, Jackson, Michigan 49202, *Established in 1916.*

Again, I suffered the roller coaster of emotions: seeing a response—feeling hopeful; reading a negative response—crashing to my too-familiar depth of depression; reactions I came to expect through the years, as well as I expected snow to fall every winter.

I presumed this letter held yet another negative response.

I opened it:

"It has taken awhile to respond to your letter, as this entailed searching through old records with very limited information. There was a Susan Marie born in what was then the maternity ward of this agency on July 18, 1954. This infant was then released for adoption by her mother.

"Based on the information you gave us, my guess is that this is a record of your birth, but obviously I cannot vouch for this without more information.

> *"There is little information in the record, other than a pregnancy record. I hope this information is helpful to you."*

Helpful? Are you serious? Nobody could have persuaded me these were *not* my records. After I mailed 137 letters to the city of Jackson, Michigan, and this was the solitary one who held a record of a Susan Marie, I had no doubt my search was near the end.

I bolted to the phone and dialed the number on the letterhead. Bug-eyed and trembling, I wasn't thinking clearly. Glancing at the clock hanging above the phone—7:00. I should have been aware the office would be empty that time of night but, teetering at the top of my roller-coaster ride, the possibility never crossed my mind.

But guess what? Someone answered.

"Can I please speak to Mrs. Roland?"

"Sure. Hold on, please."

Oh, my God—she's there!

A familiar aroma compelled me to turn towards the avocado-green stove. Greg already made dinner—his famous GB slop with sausage, onions, corn, potatoes and ketchup. Real soul-mate comfort food.

"Hello. This is Mrs. Roland. How may I help you?"

"This is Susan Beckman. I wrote you a letter asking if you had my records and wondered—"

"Yes, I remember."

"I'd like to set up a meeting with you."

"I'm not even sure if these are your records. And you know, I can't *tell* you any information."

"I'm aware of that, but I'd still like to meet with you."

"Okay. Can we set it up for tomorrow, say around 1:00?"

"Thank you so much."

The rest of that memorable evening passed like a foggy haze. I repeatedly read the letter throughout the night.

I held concrete evidence in my hands with *my* name and *my* birth date typed in black letters on white linen paper. Real proof I had been born *somewhere*.

I fell asleep with the tear-stained letter gripped in my hand.

Chapter 15

The Delivery Room

Sixty-three miles in misty fog, I pushed the gas pedal another inch and prayed flashing red lights didn't pop up in my rearview mirror.

Two miles to Exit 138. Turn left at stop light. Turn right at dead end onto Lansing Avenue. Go two blocks to the red brick building on the left.

Little white houses lined the street, with gravel alleys in between. Golden yellow leaves on maple trees. Towering evergreens mixed among massive elms. A blue aluminum-sided house. Was my mother raised in one of these homes?

Dead end. Turn right. A green Jackson City Limits sign. I drove along the same streets my mother had known back in 1954. Jackson County Health Department. Perhaps my mother went there for OB appointments when pregnant with me.

Speed limit sign—25. I glimpsed at my speedometer, I'm going 15. I wanted to savor each tree, every building, all the houses. I wanted the scenery imprinted forever in my mind so I would be able to replay it like a TV show rerun.

Then the building to my left. The place where I was born. Three stories tall, built with dark-red brick. Three gabled rooftops trimmed in beige. Windows too numerous to count. A brick chimney stood tall and straight.

A half-barren tree stood to my left as I turned into the driveway. I stopped my car in the rear parking lot. My stomach flip-flopped when I considered my mother walked upon this same property. I grabbed my purse and exited the car.

My feet were heavy like cement blocks. Curly brown leaves crunched under my shoes. Moist green moss covered parts of the sidewalk. I wondered if there was moss when my mother lived here. My hand seemed weighted down with lead when I reached to open the door. I felt drugged.

+ + +

I struggled down the hallway towards the receptionist's desk.

"I'm Susan Beckman. I have an appointment with Mrs. Roland at 1:00."

"Oh, yes. She's expecting you. I'll let her know you are here."

Mrs. Roland greeted me with a smile and stretched forth her hand to shake mine. An elderly woman with white hair, slightly overweight, and shorter than me, which was significant since I'm only five foot.

"Let me give you a tour first before we go to my office."

I couldn't respond, never expecting to stroll through the same rooms as my mother had 24 years earlier.

We entered a large room with several metal tables and folding chairs.

"Here's the lunch area where the girls eat their meals. Of course, it wasn't here when your mother was here. This part of the building was added on later. On sunny days, they'd go outside and eat at the picnic tables."

I still remained speechless. For only a second, as I looked out the window, a mirage appeared resembling a ghost-like shadow of my mother, then disappeared.

Three steps up. We entered a huge room with a fireplace and a black baby-grand piano in the corner.

"This is where the girls would meet with their families on visiting day."

The room blurred as I brushed away tears. I squinted to perceive visitations through my mother's eyes. Who in the family visited my mother in this room? Did she play the piano like me?

I blinked as Mrs. Roland spoke again.

"You know, I was here back in 1954 when you were born, although I don't remember your mother because that was so long ago and there have been many girls come through here. Let's go upstairs."

I grabbed the glossy banister, smelling of fresh wax, and buffed smooth through the ages by hands sliding along the wood. I laid my hand upon the same wood my mother touched. I anticipated a shock to shoot through my body, but instead I'm comforted by a tranquil peace, although the setting seemed a bit creepy.

Reaching the second floor, Mrs. Roland guided me to the end of the hallway with a door to our right.

The Delivery Room

"This home isn't used as a place to deliver babies any longer. The mothers are now taken to a local hospital. But back in the 1950s this room was used as the delivery room."

I repressed a sob ready to explode, as I tried to analyze this room on the day I was born…the room where my mother gave birth to me.

Back down the hall to a small open area with windows on two sides, Mrs. Roland explained, "Here's what had been the nursery back then."

I pictured myself as a newborn, lying in a bassinet, as rays of sunshine warmed my skin.

Chapter 16

The Dangling Page

Arriving at her office, she closed the door and sat across from me at her desk. As she opened a folder, I noticed a stack of 8-1/2-by-11-inch paper, with 5-by-7-inch paper stapled on top.

I watched as she removed the first staple and laid the smaller papers aside.

Grab and run, my first instinct. But which stack?

"You know, I'm not able to *tell* you any identifying information."

"I understand," and speculated if her emphasis on *tell* held any meaning.

Reaching into my purse, I gripped the

8-by-7-inch brown wire-bound notebook, purchased at Woolworth's this morning specifically for this occasion. I opened to the second page and plunged in, asking questions which had accumulated the past 24 years.

"What was my mother's occupation?"

"Student."

"How old was my mother?"

"Seventeen-and-a-half."

"How old was my father?"

"There's nothing listed for him."

"What religion was my mother? Was she Catholic?"

"I'm not showing any religion."

"Where was my mother's birthplace?"

"I'm not showing where she was born. You know I can't *tell* you any identifying information."

"What area was my mother from?"

"Uh…what county were you *adopted* in?"

"Monroe County."

"Go there," she emphasized.

Ah-ha! She didn't tell *me. Now I know how to approach this.*

But wait…I always assumed my mother lived in Jackson, since I was born there. I now embraced new information.

"Did I have any siblings at the time of my birth?"

"No."

"What were her parents' occupations?" "Did she smoke?" "How did she get here?" "Who paid for her expenses?" "Why was she here?" "Why did she give me up?"

Nothing in my chart with regard to those questions.

"I can give you the medical information, since that is considered nonidentifying."

"Okay. What time was I born?"

"3:46 a.m., with the placenta delivered at 3:50 a.m."

"How much did I weigh?"

"I don't show your birth weight."

"Was it a single birth?"

"Yes, and it was with low forceps."

"What was the length of labor?"

"Labor started at 3:00 a.m., so 46 minutes, with Dr. Richard Ries delivering."

"What kind of delivery was it?"

"She had a saddle block."

"Were there any delivery complications?"

"No."

"Did I have any noted birthmarks?"

"No."

"What was her due date?"

"Her last period was on October 18, 1953, and the due date was July 25, 1954."

"Did she have any health problems?"

"It doesn't appear so. She weighed 132 pounds on July 15th and 129-1/2 pounds when she was discharged. Her highest blood pressure was 120/80 in mid-June."

"Can you tell from her last name what nationality she was?"

"Looks like a mid-Northern Anglo-Saxon name."

"What was my mother's first name?"

"I can't tell you."

"What was my father's first name?"

"It doesn't say."

As I glanced up to look at her, she held the stack of papers straight up high, hiding her face. She deliberately flipped over the top page. It dangled in front of my face.

I blinked a couple times to confirm I hadn't imagined what I saw.

I believed the top line read *Kaye Pollock*.

I blinked again. I held my breath and tried to hold still so the cloudy letters would come into focus.

Still looked like *Kaye Pollock* to me.

She lowered the papers. With focused eye contact on Mrs. Roland, I blindly fumbled to flip through a couple pages of the notebook lying on my lap and scribbled *Kaye Pollock* on a blank page. I didn't want her to catch me writing. I swiftly looked down to see if it was legible.

My chest pinched as my heart throbbed faster and faster. I tried catching my breath so I might inhale and exhale more evenly.

Mrs. Roland's eyes latched onto mine. I thanked her with a slim smile. She did not break the law to *tell* me anything. But she sure as heck *showed* me.

I now *owned* a name.

"How long was my mother here?"

"She was seven months pregnant when she came here and she left in September, two months after your birth, so she was here a total of four months."

"Why was I given up for adoption?"

"It was a voluntary relinquishment. Your mother signed the papers. However, there isn't a reason in the file."

"Did she have any siblings?"

"Yes, six; two brothers and four sisters."

"Have any relatives contacted you?"

"No."

"Has my mother contacted you?"

"No."

"Who came to get me?"

"I'm not allowed to *tell* you."

"Okay. I guess that's all the questions I have. Thank you so much, Mrs. Roland, for your time. You have no idea how much I appreciate it."

We shook hands.

+ + +

I wanted to run, but slowed my stride and concentrated. When my feet touched the parking lot, my pace increased.

I needed to get out of here quickly. I didn't want to get arrested for learning information which was against the law, even if it's as simple as a name. *My* last name. The one thing I should be entitled to, but the law says I can't have it.

Lansing, Michigan. Thirty-nine miles north of Jackson. I couldn't drive fast enough. I now realized I'd be able to obtain my original birth certificate because I knew my last name.

Pollock. Susan Marie Pollock.

The Vital Statistics office had to be downtown. I never visited Lansing before, but follow the signs and I'd get there.

My keen sense of direction played in my favor. I don't know how I did it with my disoriented state of mind, but I opened the door and stepped inside.

"I need a copy of my birth certificate, please."

Cheryl, from my adoption support group, told me to never mention adoption; just fill out the paperwork as if nothing is unusual.

"Complete this application over at the counter and bring it back here."

Carefully printing my mother's name, Kaye

Pollock, and *my* name, Susan Marie Pollock, I filled in my date of birth, July 18, 1954, and place of birth, Jackson, Michigan.

Weird, writing my name for the first time as Pollock.

I left father's name blank.

Handing the application to the clerk behind the frosted glass window, along with a check, she inspected the piece of paper.

Please, God, don't let her figure out this is for my original birth certificate.

"Everything looks good. We'll mail you a copy in four to six weeks."

Oh. My. God. The walls caved in around me.

I forced a smile and thanked her. How would I find the strength to survive from day to day until then?

In between the daily encounter with my mailbox, I kept myself busy and continued on with my search as best as I knew how. I couldn't idly sit and wait. I pushed on to do something productive.

I sat at the kitchen table each night. I called every Pollock in the Monroe phone book.

"I'm trying to locate a relative by the name of Kaye Pollock, K-A-Y-E."

"I'm sorry, there's no one in our family with that name."

Chapter 17

Three-Foot Long Drawers

"Who's Aleda Fay Pollock?" I questioned, two weeks after applying for my original birth certificate.

Holding the shiny black Certificate of Live Birth in my hand, I double-checked:

Child's Name – Susan Marie Pollock.

Mother of Child – Aleda Fay Pollock.

Not Kaye, but Aleda Fay.

Had she gone by a different first name at the unwed mother's home? Or had I misread the name on the papers? It didn't matter.

Date of birth – July 18, 1954.

Place of birth – Jackson, Michigan.

I reverently slid my fingers back and forth over my name, Susan Marie Pollock.

Yep. This is me.

But how bizarre I now held two of my very own birth certificates with two different names.

Where do I go from here?

I called the leader of my adoption support group.

"Cheryl, I just got my original birth certificate. You aren't gonna believe this. Her first name isn't Kaye, it's Aleda Fay. I was going by the wrong first name all along."

"Wow. Well, at least now you have the correct name."

"What do I do now? How do I find her?"

"Okay. You have to assume she's married by now, so her last name of Pollock would have changed. Since she has two brothers, you know their last names will be the same. You need to find one of her brothers."

"How in the world—"

"Don't worry. It's not as difficult as you think. The library has death indexes. You'll need to go through all the Pollocks. Read the obituaries and look at the survivors. If you can find Aleda listed as a survivor, any other names will be her siblings."

+ + +

Shady gingko trees still lined the sidewalk leading to the library door on this golden Saturday morning. I turned the same heavy doorknob I touched as a child.

The musty smell of dusty, old books stirred up blissful childhood memories. I never dreamed I would enter the doors of this library as an adult to search for my birth mother.

"Where can I find the death index records?"

"Second floor, to your left."

Wood cabinets with miniature drawers lined the walls and filled the room.

Another librarian. Another question. Another nauseating stomach.

"I'd like to find the death indexes for anyone with the last name of Pollock."

I hoped it wasn't obvious who I wanted to find. I felt sneaky and didn't want to get caught. Surveying the room, I confirmed no one watched me. Touching my hair, I fluffed my bangs; I didn't want the librarian to see *adopted* stamped across my forehead.

"What is the year of death?"

"Ummm…I don't know. I just want to search for any Pollock who is deceased."

"Okay. The index is not filed alphabetically. They are filed by the year of death for the past 60 years. The number in the upper right-hand corner of the card gives the book number where the obituary can be found. Those books are in the next room right over there."

"Okay."

"If you need anything else, let me know."

Clutching my worn notebook, I claimed an empty table. I tried to think of the best angle to approach this search.

I pulled out the three-foot long drawer labeled 1937 and carried it to my table. Search for Pollock, write down the first name, date of death, and the book number where the obituary is filed.

Then read the obituaries to look for my mother as a survivor, trying to find one of her brother's names.

Pollock. Pollock. Pollock.

Date of death, October 14, 1937
Glee Pollock
Book Number 26

Ten drawers later:

Eliza Pollock
June 4, 1938,
Book Number 74

Twenty-one drawers:

Daniel Pollock
date of death June 13, 1939
Book Number 333

Forty-seven:

March 24, 1965
Nora M. Pollock
Book Number 713

I filled six pages in my notebook. Now to find matching obituaries. Two hours until the library closed.

Forty-five minutes and 68 obituaries later, I matched Daniel Pollock with his obituary; "Born April 3, 1933, to Sanger and Elizabeth," (wow, my youngest daughter's day of birth) "died June 13, 1939, age 6, cause of death meningitis."

How sad. Six years old.

Skimming to survivors, "At home, Leonard, Sanger, Jr., Irwin Lee, Viola, Anna May, and Aleda."

Aleda.

My mom. That's her. There can't be many other people in Monroe with the first name of Aleda.

Her parents, Sanger and Elizabeth Pollock—my grandparents. Her brothers, Leonard, Sanger, Jr., and Irwin Lee—my uncles.

Flipping through my notebook, I didn't notice a Sanger Pollock listed in the death index. Maybe he didn't die in Monroe.

Ten minutes until closing, I rushed to the Monroe phone book. Pollock—no listing for Sanger, Leonard or Irwin.

"Where can I find a death index for

somewhere outside of Monroe?"

"You need to contact Vital Statistics in Lansing, but they won't be open until Monday."

+ + +

Arriving to work at 8:00, one more hour until the office opened in Lansing. I worked, but don't ask me what I typed because my mind was busy constructing a phone call.

"I'm trying to find a death certificate for my grandfather."

"What's the date of death?"

"I'm not sure, but I know it was after 1939. His name was Sanger Pollock."

"We show a Sanger D. Pollock, age 67, died November 22, 1960, in Ann Arbor, Michigan."

"Do you have any other information?"

"Yes, ma'am. You can call the Ann Arbor Courthouse to request a death certificate. Here's their phone number."

Two minutes later, I spoke with the clerk.

"How do I go about getting a death

certificate for my grandfather?"

I don't feel guilty. This time I'm not lying. I'm telling the truth. This really is for my own grandfather.

"I can look it up for you right now."

I stuttered, not prepared to write anything.

"Uh…okay. You c-c-can give me the information n-n-now?"

"I sure can. What is the name and date of death?"

"Sanger D. Pollock, November 22, 1960."

"His birthdate was December 28, 1892. Cause of death was bronchial lobar pneumonia. Age 67. Funeral Home in Dundee, Michigan, was R. F. Fisher, with burial in Ligonier, Indiana."

"Thank you so much."

"Do you want the name of the informant?"

"Oh…all right…I guess."

What good will that do me? It's probably just a doctor at the hospital.

"The informant was a Dr. Leland Pollock, New Haven, Indiana."

My eyes opened wider. My body stiffened.

"Anything else I can help you with today?"

"No. Thank you so very much."

Leland. Close to Leonard. My uncle. My uncle was the informant for my grandfather's death information.

"I'd like the number for a Dr. Leland Pollock in New Haven."

"Do you want the office or the residence?"

"Both, please."

+ + +

"Could I please speak to Dr. Leland Pollock?"

"Speaking."

"I'm working on a family tree and I'm trying to find your sister, Aleda."

"Oh, she's only my half-sister. I haven't kept in touch with her for years."

My back slouched.

If he knows I'm adopted, he's not going to tell me anything.

"Okay. Is there anyone else in the family who might help?"

"Sure. My other sister in Detroit would know where Aleda is. They keep in touch with each other. Hold on while I get her phone number."

My leg shook. I tapped my foot. My throat tightened.

"Her name is Anna May Stewart. She's married to Hank Szatkowski, but they go by the stage name of Stewart. They play in a band. They live near Hazel Park, Michigan. Here's her phone number."

Hazel Park. Only 60-some miles north of me.

Anna May. One of my mom's sisters listed in the obituary. My aunt.

Chapter 18

Deer Hunting

"Cheryl, I have my aunt's phone number. What do I tell her? I don't know what to do."

"Don't tell her who you are. You can start off by telling her that you are with an attorney's office. Make up a name. Tell her you are probating a will and you need to locate Aleda Pollock. She might give you the information right off the bat."

"What do I do if she doesn't?"

"Then you can slowly go into a little more detail. Give your name, tell her you haven't met, and ask if she's free to talk. Just play it by ear. Don't worry, it'll come to you what to say."

My lunch hour wasted. I dialed my aunt's phone number 33 times. No answer.

Through the afternoon I called every 10 minutes. After four hours, I swiveled my chair around to face the wall of windows. I blindly gazed at the Toledo skyline from the 13th floor of my office. Somewhere north of where I sat was my aunt—the only connection to my mother.

Where was she? Why isn't she home answering her phone? She's missing a very important phone call. What would I do if she never answered?

Wait…maybe she works. That's it. She must be working and won't be home until after 5:00.

I wasn't able to sort through my muddled thoughts, like flipping a deck of cards into the air and watching them flutter to the floor, landing every which way.

The clock displayed 5:37. One last try before I leave the office this Friday evening.

"Hello?"

"Could I please speak to Anna Stewart?"

"Who is this?"

"I work for Attorney Greg Beckman and we are probating a will. We need to locate Aleda

Pollock."

"Why do you need to contact Aleda?"

"We are trying to get in touch with her because of a will."

"Who did you say you were again?"

"This is Attorney Greg Beckman's office."

"I don't know anyone by that name."

I looked at the ceiling tiles, yellowed by cigarette smoke.

"We need to locate your sister, Aleda."

"Why do you need to find her? What does she have to do with anything?"

"She is mentioned in the will. We need to locate her to close this estate?"

"Why am I not mentioned in the will? Are you sure my name isn't there?"

I pressed my fingers to my forehead and rolled my eyes.

"I don't know, but Aleda is mentioned. Can you tell me where she is?"

"I'm not telling you anything until you tell me who you are."

I paced behind my desk as far away as the telephone cord would allow.

"I'm with an attorney's office."

"What is your name? Who are you?"

"I work for Attorney Greg Beckman."

"And I want to know why I ain't listed in this will."

"We just need to locate Aleda."

"Where are you calling from?"

I stepped to the edge of glass windows which stretched from the ceiling to floor. As I looked down 13 floors at trees with leafless branches, my fingers chilled and went numb.

"Listen. I don't know what's going on, but I'm not gonna tell you anything and I'm definitely not going to tell you where Aleda is until I find out what's going on here."

What do I do? She's gonna hang up. It's now or never.

"Does the date *July 18, 1954*, mean anything to you?"

"Nope, sure doesn't."

"Was anyone in your family born on that date?"

"Nobody in the family has that birthday."

I gulped.

"Did Aleda ever have a baby and give it up for adoption?"

"Oh, my God, no. Aleda would never do that. One of my other sisters might have done something like that, but *never* Aleda."

"Never?"

"Nope, she'd never do that."

I sat and watched as twinkling lights appeared in windows across town.

"I'm the baby she gave up for adoption."

Within the sound of silence, I closed my eyes and prayed. My aunt wept softly.

"Oh, my God, you're my niece."

Tears tickled my cheeks and formed dark oval blotches on my blue denim skirt.

"Do you have a crooked smile?"

"Yes, I do."

"So does Aleda. How tall are you?"

"Five foot. What does she look like?"

"She's very pretty, about five-foot four. She's married to Bill Coverdale, they have six children and live in California."

As our conversation continued, I noticed the darkness of black sky. The streetlights flashed on.

"But I'm *still* not gonna give you any more information or tell you where she is in California."

"Okay. Can you contact her for me and let her know I was looking for her?"

"Sure, I'll do that. Listen, we're leaving town tomorrow to go deer hunting. I'll call you when we get back in a couple weeks."

Deer hunting is more important than putting me in touch with my birth mother?

I didn't have a choice. My new-found aunt—the single link to my mother.

How would I survive the next couple weeks awaiting that phone call?

Chapter 19

Your Cheatin' Heart

Friday nights I looked forward to relaxing. But I couldn't sit still. The conversation with my aunt replayed in my head. I recited it to my husband over and over.

I cannot wait two weeks. My search can't stop. It must move forward. I grabbed my notebook and ran upstairs. My husband followed.

"What are you doing now?"

"I'm going to find her. My aunt said she lives in California. I have her husband's name."

"What makes you think you'll find her in the whole state of California if you don't even know what town she lives in?"

"I'll call the 411 Information in every town in California, if I have to. It's 7:00 here, but it's only 4:00 there. I still have about five hours to call her when I get a phone number."

"You're nuts. You're never gonna find her that way. Why don't you wait until your aunt calls back in a couple weeks?"

"I can't. I can't wait. I have to do something productive. I've come this far. I'm not going to waste a night without trying to find her. I feel like she's so close, yet so far away."

Six hours later, with stinging, heavy-laden eyes, my husband convinced me to go to bed.

+ + +

Saturday, November 18th, I sat in my blue plaid flannel jammas and watched cartoons with my girls.

The phone rang. My heart sank. I dashed upstairs.

"Hi. This is Penny. I'm calling to remind you of the Family Life meeting at church tomorrow night."

"We'll be there. Thanks for calling, Penny."

Tucking my feet underneath the red and black crocheted afghan, I settled back upon the couch.

The phone rang. My heart tapped in double-beats. I flew to the kitchen again.

"Hey, Sue. This is Judy. How are you holding up?"

"Oh, Judy, I don't know how I'm gonna make it. My heart sinks when the phone rings. I can't believe my aunt would make me wait two weeks."

I slouched, sat down, laid my head back on a pillow.

What if my aunt tried calling while I was on the phone a minute ago? What if the phone isn't working now?

Racing upstairs, two steps at a time, I lifted the receiver—the steady buzz of a dial tone.

Traipsing back downstairs, I plopped onto the rocker, reassured.

RING – RING.

I moaned, "Am I going to have this feeling every time the phone rings for the next two weeks?"

I bolted.

"Hello?"

"Hi, Susan. This is your Aunt Ann."

I collapsed onto the kitchen chair.

"Hi. How are you?"

"I contacted your mother last night. She was glad to hear you were looking for her."

"Really?"

"But I'm *still* not telling you where she is. I need to see you first."

"I'd be happy to meet with you." I ripped a blank page from my notebook and grabbed a pen.

"When can you come up here?"

"Well, as soon as I can shower and get in the car."

"Okay. That sounds good. I'll give you directions to our house. It should take you about an hour to drive here."

The shaking in my hand traveled towards

my shoulder and my heart quivered.

"I'll let my husband write down the directions."

I threw the BIC pen at him and pointed to the blank paper on the table.

I burped, but really wanted to puke.

+ + +

Our 1968 white Opal station wagon sputtered 10 miles north of Toledo. The heater broke. We pulled to the side of I-75. The engine pinged as the carburetor fell off. My husband wrestled to screw it back on.

Snowflakes gracefully danced about through the frigid air.

Please, Lord, we have to get there. If ever You are going to answer a prayer, please answer this one.

The girls huddled together on the back seat. We struggled to stay warm during the remaining 50-mile ride.

Pulling into the driveway of a small suburban white house, my aunt stepped onto their front porch. I hesitated.

Would I be accepted? Did she believe I'm Aleda's daughter?

She grinned. I walked towards her. She stepped closer to me and opened her arms. We hugged and cried.

"You look just like your mother."

As I stepped into the toasty living room, I trembled and tried to rid the chill from my bones, as Uncle Hank hugged me tight.

"I'm *still* not telling you where your mother is. Have a seat. I need to explain some things first."

Oh, no. She doesn't want anything to do with me. This must be bad if it needs an explanation.

She laid a photo album with a burgundy cover in my lap, opening to a page.

"Here's some pictures of your mother."

Breathless, I softly laid my right hand upon the yellowed, brittle plastic covering the photos. I used my left hand to swiftly brush away tears so they didn't drip and distort my mother's image.

Motionless, I'm disoriented as I viewed a photo of my mother for the first time. Part of me.

I'm part of her. We are one, as if my lingering hand in contact with the photo allowed her presence to flow into me.

If she doesn't want to see me, that's fine. I'm ready for whatever happens. I've at least seen a picture of her now.

Eager to see more, I gingerly turned pages, while my aunt explained.

"I needed to see you in person to be sure you were really Aleda's daughter. You see, we have a half-sister who's mean and vindictive. We thought somebody was trying to play a joke on us. I needed to see you first to make sure it was really you. Your mother was tricked into signing your adoption papers by our sister."

It didn't matter to me anymore why I was given up for adoption. I found her. I'm looking at pictures of her. Nothing else existed in my world at that moment.

We hugged, cried, talked, laughed and looked at pictures as my aunt introduced me to the rest of my family in the album.

"I told your mother I'd call her after I met you."

No answer. She called again. No answer. Seven hours later. No answer.

"I just don't understand." My aunt shook her head, bewildered. "She knew I was gonna call her today. With six kids at home, there's always someone to answer the phone."

Uncle Hank strummed his guitar and tried to lighten the gloomy mood which mingled with our cigarette smoke clouding the room.

Aunt Ann made sandwiches and we waited.

Nine hours later, with the aftertaste of tuna fish and onions on my tongue, Aunt Ann screamed into the phone.

"Aleda, where have you been? We've been trying to call you all day. What's going on?"

She relayed to us that my mother's phone had been disconnected. They tried all day to convince the phone company to at least allow incoming calls.

"I have your daughter sitting here next to me. She's beautiful. She looks exactly like you. Would you like to talk to her?"

A short convulsive inhale of air preceded my groan. I listened to the same through the phone, as my fingers squeezed the receiver.

As we huddled around the sparkly Formica table in the kitchen, Uncle Hank played and sang *Your Cheatin' Heart*.

"...make you weep, you'll cry and cry..."

My shoulders shook as I sobbed.

"...when tears come down, like falling rain..."

My aunt shoved a wad of Kleenex into my hand.

"...you'll walk the floor...and call my name..."

I strained to catch a sound of my mother calling my name.

"...and crave the love you threw away..."

I don't care if she threw me away. I don't care what the circumstances were with my adoption.

Two hours later, I couldn't release my grip off the phone. I held the only link to what I'd been looking for the past 24 years.

I can't let go, now that I found it.

Chapter 20

Covering the Bases

I couldn't jump for joy in front of my parents on Thanksgiving in 1978.

Finding my birth mom was like searching for years for a missing diamond ring. You receive a call informing you the ring was found. You can't contain your excitement over a long-lost jewel. You want to share your joy and express how lucky you are. At long last you look forward to holding this jewel in your hand.

You want to shout to everyone you meet, including the stranger behind the cash register at K-Mart.

My life's different, though. I can't share the joy with my parents. I'm constantly on guard. I made a conscious effort to seriously consider each word before I spoke. Don't let my joy spill over. If only…if only my parents would be like other adoptive parents at my support group who helped their adopted child search for their birth family. But they weren't. Caution is the world I lived in now.

One more week and I'd see my birth mother face to face.

Time ticked in slow motion, but my mind labored in whirlwind overtime. I attempted to cover all my bases, except this wasn't a baseball game. There's more than three to cover in this situation.

My mom and I both remained agitated with anticipation. The plan was she'd fly into Detroit. I would meet her, spend the night at Aunt Ann's and go home the next day. She'd stay with Aunt Ann and Uncle Hank the first week. She wanted to visit with them—get her nerves settled.

This is one nervous lady. I want to spend time with her and get to know her. Now I have to wait another week after meeting her before that will happen.

I'd pick her up and she'd stay with us the second week. My husband and girls would meet her for the first time.

+ + +

"Greg, how are we gonna keep the girls from telling my parents about their *other* Grandma?"

"I don't know, Honey. But we need to come up with something. If they find out, they'll never talk to us again."

Lies. They always worked in my favor before.

My birth mom wanted our girls to call her Nanny. Simple. They called Greg's mom Nanny and my mom Grandma. If they mentioned the name Nanny, we could brush it off as if they are referring to Greg's mom.

One base covered. And the lies begin again.

"What happens if my parents call when I'm gone the one night at Aunt Ann's with my mom?"

"Uh......."

"I know. You can tell them I'm at a church meeting or whatever. Make up something."

Second base covered. More lies.

My parents lived in Tecumseh, Michigan, 45 miles north of Toledo.

"Well, at least your parents don't come to see us, so they won't appear on our doorstep for a surprise visit."

"Yeah. That's true."

Third base covered. No lie involved with this one.

"And you don't talk to them on the phone very often. So you could go the whole week she's here and not worry about talking to you parents."

"But what if they happen to call and hear her voice in the background?"

"Susan, I really don't think—"

"But what if…I know…I could tell them a friend stopped by."

Fourth base covered.

"What if the girls say something later to my parents about a lady staying at our house for more than one day?"

"I don't know, Susan. What do you think?"

"It might work if I tell my parents ahead of time we have a friend from the Air Force coming to visit."

"Okay. But it's up to you."

Fifth base covered. And the lies continued.

+ + +

"I've been talking to Aunt Ann. She's adamant about getting the TV station and newspaper at the airport to do a story about my mom and I meeting for the first time."

"Oh, my God, Susan. You can't let her do that."

"I know. Tecumseh isn't too far from Detroit. The *Detroit Free Press* is a big newspaper and maybe my parents subscribe to it."

"Even if they don't, what if one of their friends might see the newspaper write-up and tell them?"

"Plus, if it's on TV, I know my parents get the channel from Detroit. They would see it. I can't let that happen."

I begged and pleaded with Aunt Ann to not have the media at the airport. I explained I didn't want my parents to find out.

It's my own selfish desire which brought my birth mom and I together. I didn't want anyone hurt because of my greediness.

"Aunt Ann, we can't have the TV or newspaper at the airport. Someone might see it and tell my parents."

"Well, we have to do something. I'm proud you found your mom. I want everyone to know about it."

"I understand. But you have to understand something, like this could ruin my relationship with my parents. I can't risk it."

"Okay. What if we have our small-town newspaper here at my house to do a short interview? That paper is only delivered to our little community."

"All right. I guess it's okay."

Am I able to pull this off without causing misery?

Chapter 21

Loretta Lynn

What do you wear at age 24 when meeting your mother for the first time? Rummaging through my closet, I couldn't decide.

"Greg, what should I wear? I don't know what to wear."

"Honey, it doesn't matter because she—"

"It *does* matter. She hasn't seen me since I was a baby. Darn it, I don't know what to wear."

What if I'm too fat? I never learned my birth weight, but I guessed I've gained at least 105 pounds since then. I don't want to look fat.

I chose a stretch knit top with pastel-colored stripes, along with long black slacks.

Greg and the girls stayed home.

I rode with Aunt Ann and Uncle Hank to the Detroit airport. People everywhere. Mobs of people dashed past me. Bumped my elbow. Brushed against my shoulder. A white Samsonite suitcase banged my knee.

What if my mom got here early and we missed her?

I searched faces in the swarming herd of strangers. We waited at the gate.

Waiting. Waiting. Waiting.

"When is her plane gonna land?"

My aunt stretched her arm around my shoulder to comfort me.

"Let's stand over here so we aren't so near the door when she gets off the plane. I know my sister. She's a very nervous person. Give her a chance to let it sink in when she sees you."

I inspected my surroundings. No TV cameras, that I noticed. Maybe they're hidden. My aunt might have been sneaky and called the TV station anyway. If I see anything resembling the media, I'll spin and run. Blend in with the crowd.

My stomach heaved. I can't let my parents discover what I've done.

I examined faces again. If I noticed a familiar face of someone who might know my parents, I'm out of here.

On guard. Be on guard.

"Flight 1706 now arriving from Los Angeles at Gate 36."

Strange people exited and filed through the doorway.

Oh, my God. What if I don't know who she is? That would be humiliating if I don't recognize my own mother.

"Aunt Ann, will you tell me when she gets—"

"There she is, Susan. There's your mother."

I stiffened. Fixated upon the woman slumped against the doorway.

"Hank, go help her. She's about to pass out."

I should be the one to run to her side. I'm her daughter. She needs help. I can't let her fall.

She's going to faint. Oh, my God.

But I'm glued to the floor. I couldn't do anything but stand and stare.

Loretta Lynn. She looked young and beautiful. She looked like Loretta Lynn, with long black hair pulled up into Grecian curls, which trailed over the shoulders of her light blue silk blouse.

Aunt Ann nudged my back with her hand and walked beside me towards my mother. I looked into the slate-blue eyes of the woman who gave birth to me. This is my mother.

Wendy has her eyes. Now we know.

We grabbed one another and sobbed. Our grip enmeshed so tight, we couldn't let go.

Trembling. Her body shivered as if we stood in below-zero weather in a snow blizzard.

She leaned aside to look at my face. "You look more like him than you do me."

Uncle Hank guided us to a chair. Every few seconds we'd pull away and look at each other.

Flesh and blood. Yes, we are related.

She hugged me and cried. I sat on her lap and cried. She rocked me. And rocked me. And rocked.

Okay. Now this is getting uncomfortable. I don't like this. How can I pull away and stop this rocking without hurting her feelings?

Then I remembered Cheryl, the support group leader, when she explained to me what might happen.

"Don't be surprised if she just wants to hold you. Remember, the last time she saw you was when she cradled you in her arms as a tiny newborn. In her mind, you haven't grown up because the last image she has of you is a baby. Let her have this time of holding you, if that's what she wants."

My tension eased. I relaxed. No TV cameras buzzed. No newspaper reporters aimed and clicked cameras. None of my parents' friends witnessed this reunion.

Only me and my mom. That's all who existed at Gate 36 in the Detroit airport.

Chapter 22

Pulled Apart

During the ride from the airport to Aunt Ann's house, my mom gripped my hand. She stared at me in a daze. I squirmed and swallowed.

This is too much closeness. I feel smothered.

We settled on the couch prepared for a long night of talking.

"You look more like him than you do me."

"Who's my birth father?"

"I don't remember his name. That whole ordeal was so traumatic, I just blocked it all out of my mind."

"What did he look like?"

"He was handsome. He had dark hair and dark eyes, like you. He had a big nose, too. You could be your father's twin, you look so much like him."

"And you don't even remember his first name?"

"Like I said, I blocked that out of my mind. I don't remember. I don't even want to talk about him."

Okay. I don't know if I believe this. How can you forget the name of a guy who got you pregnant? But I'll leave it at that. She doesn't want to talk about it. I don't want to upset her. I found her and that's enough. I'm not interested in looking for him anyway.

"I need to explain the circumstances with your adoption."

"Okay."

"My mom died in a car crash when I was 12 years old. There were so many of us kids and my dad – your grandfather – couldn't take care of us all. He put me in foster care and I became a ward of the state. I was in and out of foster homes all through my teenage years.

"I dated this guy – your biological father –

and when I found out I was pregnant and told him, he took off. I heard he was engaged to someone else and she was pregnant, too. My dad went after him and got him to pay the hospital bills.

"At that time I was living with my half-sister, Viola. She had me put in an unwed mother's home. After you were born, we weren't allowed to go into the nursery or hold the babies. But some lady there at the home let me take pictures every day and they let me go in there to hold you.

"Since I was a ward of the state, they wouldn't let me keep you unless I had a job and a place to stay. So they put you in one of them foster homes. We couldn't visit the baby there. They were afraid the girl would take off with the baby. I got a job as a waitress and the owners of the restaurant let me live in a basement apartment.

"In the meantime, Viola brought papers to me. She said you was sick and I needed to sign them papers in order for you to get treated. I was young and stupid. I didn't read the papers. I just went ahead and signed them.

"After I got settled in my apartment and started my waitressing job, a couple weeks later I went back to get you. I found out I had signed adoption papers. They had tricked me. I really did want to keep you. And I tried. But they tricked me into signing them papers. I ain't lying to you,

Sweetie.

"That's why your Aunt Ann here needed to meet you first after you found me. We thought Vi was playing a game with us.

"Then I met your father, Bill—"

"Wait. My father, Bill?"

"That's my husband. He's as much your dad as anyone."

This is getting weird. I've never met this guy and now she wants me to consider him my dad?

"We got married and had six kids. We tried and tried to find you. I wanted to get you back. But nobody would tell us nothing."

We went to bed at two a.m. I had to return back home the next day.

+ + +

The next morning I entered the living room. I giggled.

"Oh, my God. I can't believe this. We're both wearing red tops."

The first of many-to-come coincidences.

We sat next to each other and looked through more photos. My mom kicked off her shoes. She bent her big toes under her foot and cracked them. Another trait of something I've done all my life.

Genetic? Environmental? Hard to tell the difference.

+ + +

I returned to Aunt Ann's the following week to bring my mom to our house.

The small-town newspaper reporter interviewed us and snapped pictures. I'm confident this story will appear in only one insignificant newspaper outside the Detroit area.

The reporter asked my mom, "What do you want for the future?"

"Oh, Susan and her family are gonna move to California. They're already making plans. We'll finally be together. I'll have my daughter with me again—the daughter who was taken from me."

Wait. What? I'm moving to California?

I didn't respond. I couldn't accept that

statement in my mind. This is something we needed to talk about. We can't move. I don't *want* to move to California. But I'll let her dwell on that fantasy for now.

My stomach swished, like I had motion sickness, as her statement floated in my mind like dirty smog which you can't see through.

+ + +

My mom spent a week with us. Our girls loved her. She read them stories, hugged them, enjoyed them. She fit right in with our family.

"When can you come to California to meet your brothers and sister?"

"They really want to meet me? Did they know about me?"

"Oh, yes. We didn't keep nothing from them. They knowed all about you when they was growing up. They always wanted to find you some day. I cried every year when it was your birthday."

She remembered.

"I tried finding you. I talked to Vi's friends and babysitters to see if they knew where you was. After I married Bill, we put ads in newspapers. And just last year we talked to a lawyer. But they couldn't do nothing.

"Now, I want to hear about your life. Them people that adopted you."

"I had a very good life."

"I'm glad you were happy. I always wondered if they treated you right."

"I grew up with a brother and a sister. They adopted my brother and then had my sister."

"Well, now you have six more."

"This will be hard to get used to. I'm having a hard time just remembering their names."

"Do them people know you found me?"

"No, they don't. They never wanted to talk much about my adoption or me searching for you. They figured they were my parents and they didn't talk about my birth family."

"Oh, Susan, that's too bad. I ain't never had hard feelings toward them. I hope they don't hate me."

"I'm sure they don't. But we just never talked about it."

I don't want to talk too much about my adoptive parents. I can't hurt her feelings. I'm torn between pleasing my adoptive parents and my birth mom.

Chapter 23

California Here We Come

January 1979. Plans in place.

I told my parents we'd be flying to California to visit friends we knew from the Air Force.

More lies.

Adoptees never knew what they'd find in a birth family. Lots of bizarre images popped into my head.

I'd grown up with a brother and a sister. I wasn't searching for more, but knew if there happened to be any, I'd love them just the same. I'm open-minded to accept anything.

Eager to meet my six siblings, even though

they are half-siblings, I naturally considered them my brothers and sisters. I'm ready to accept all of them, whether they accepted me or not.

Exiting the plane in Los Angeles, I met my mom's husband, Bill—although they still insisted I call him *Dad*. My first impression—Willie Nelson.

We entered their house. Christmas decorations adorned the living room, with wrapped presents stacked under the tree. They wanted to celebrate with us, so they postponed their Christmas until our visit in January.

"Here's your brothers and sister; Jack, Billy, Trudy, and Ronny. Your sister, Fayann, is married and lives in Texas. She's only 20 months younger than you. And Paul is in a nursing home because he got spinal meningitis as a baby. Someday you'll get to meet them."

Through the week, I heard several times, "I'm as much your dad as anyone. You'll call me Dad. You hear me?"

I don't want to call him Dad. I already have a Dad. I'm being forced to do this. But I'm always struggling to not hurt their feelings, so I'll go along with their wishes, even if I'm uncomfortable.

I faced a rude awakening in California—a

radically different lifestyle than I'd been raised in.

Rednecks? I didn't know what a redneck was then. But I'm afraid I'd learn real soon.

Pickup trucks in various stages of repair scattered across the yard, flowing onto the dirt road. Kids darted through the house, slamming doors and yelling. Food fights, practical jokes—all things I'm not used to.

Amidst the contrasting lifestyle, my rebellious genetic genes seemed oddly comfortable, but my environmental upbringing restrained me from getting in trouble. For some reason I fit in with these people. This is how I would have behaved if my birth mom had kept me.

+ + +

Our second day in California, Billy startled me as he sprung off the couch and bolted outside. Jack followed. Clouds of desert dust whipped around like a tornado. Frenzy everywhere. I glimpsed an occasional flailing foot or arm. Chaos.

"Greg, what's going on?"

"Susan, stay out of it. Your brothers are fighting with a boy who showed up on a bicycle."

I wrung my hands. "A fight? Somebody has

to stop them. They're gonna get hurt."

This is the first time I witnessed any physical violence. My adrenaline rushed. I kind of enjoyed the excitement, although I wasn't familiar with this type of activity. I've always been kind of a rebel. Must be in my hillbilly blood. I blended right in with their craziness. But my husband knew how to subdue me. He protected my hidden wild side from bursting forth.

But rough-and-tumble fist fights, a house surrounded by a junkyard, and other illegal incidents occurred, things I'd never been exposed to my entire life. But I still loved them all. They were blood.

When searching, I imagined too many freakish scenarios, so I'm prepared for pretty much anything. I accepted them for who they are.

I ignored their dark side.

I relished acting silly like a kid again. I'm now part of a family with lots of brothers and sisters. But the opposite lifestyle rubbed against my heart. Part of me loved being able to act myself. It's as if all along my genes joked with each other. Then my other restrained self—the part from environment—kept repeating I shouldn't be acting this way. I should be mature. I needed to control myself.

A double personality? Is this why I'm comfortable behaving one way—the "redneck" way—but confused because I knew I should be acting another way?

I tried not to think about it because I only wanted to enjoy the time with my birth mother.

+ + +

Jack is talented. He's funny. He has a big heart. He would do anything for anybody. He'd go to any length necessary to help anyone, legal or not. We got along well from the beginning.

Trudy is friendly, yet I sensed she forced herself to act nice. I didn't blame her at all. I recognized her reaction. Here I am, the oldest, who hasn't been in their life for 24 years. All of a sudden I show up. Now I'm the main attraction. I didn't want the attention. I never wanted to be set apart now, just as I didn't want to be labeled special. I simply hoped to blend in—not be treated any different.

How could anyone not love Billy? He's cute, with blue eyes and dimples. He loved horses, just like me. The one exception, he was raised around horses. He breaks horses. He rides donkeys and participates in the rodeo. He's fearless.

Ronny is the youngest—blond hair and shy. He's usually outside with his friends. I didn't spend enough time with him to really get to know him. But I knew as he grew older, we'd find the time.

Many years later I met Fayann Marie. *Is it funny she has the same middle name?* She's not like the rest of them. She's more like me—the restrained me. And God bonded us together to become sisters, to the point one would assume we'd grown up together. We are best friends. I love her most of all.

Random comments from family members confirmed that I had been the lucky one. I listened to stories from my siblings which described their childhood as so dysfunctional, they were jealous of me because I was the one who'd been adopted. They wished it had been them.

+ + +

"Come on, Susan. I've got an appointment at my hairdresser to have our hair done. I want her to do your hair the same as mine."

"Okay. If that's what you want."

"Jenny, I want you to meet Susan. Remember I told you about my daughter who was stole from me? This is her."

I allowed my mom to have fun with me. I played along with her wishes. She introduced me to all her friends as her daughter, which warmed my heart.

I drank in their local bars, danced to country western music booming from the jukebox, not inhibited at all. I'd been brought up with classical music, but country pulsated within my blood. I loved the best of both worlds.

One bar, one night, dim lights, the blue haze of cigarette smoke swirled through the atmosphere. Walking out the door with Greg, my mom, Bill, and Alan, a friend of theirs who is a police officer, I heard someone mention that Viola was sitting at the bar.

What? THE *Viola who tricked my mom into signing my adoption papers?*

I turned around and re-entered the bar. My wild side bubbled, like an overheated radiator ready to boil over. I was gonna make my presence known. Six steps inside, fingers grabbed the back of my blouse. Alan dragged me away before my crazy actions resulted in trouble.

Was it a good thing God plucked me from this lifestyle? One might say so.

And among all these new experiences, I

stepped into new relationships.

"You'll move to California. We'll be a family."

Move to California from Ohio? Why do they keep assuming we're gonna move to California? I didn't want this. But I can't tell them. Again, I don't want to hurt anyone.

I don't believe I'd be at ease living around Bill. I'm not scared or anything. But I was never exposed to their way of life. I accepted him with no problem, although many times I found myself raising my eyebrows, shaking my head.

After we returned home to Ohio, our kinship flourished through phone calls and letters.

Satisfied within myself, I cherished the joy of finding the missing part of me—my birth mom. But saddened when I couldn't share the joy with my adoptive parents.

What I never anticipated was the struggle with two families. I attempted to appease both. I straddled in the center of two opposing worlds, tried to keep my balance while being torn between two contrasting cultures. I can't blend into both worlds, much like water won't mix with oil.

+ + +

But now we had another base to cover. Our girls talked about Nanny in California.

Amy was four years old and Wendy two-and-a-half. They were still young enough that I attempted to plant lies into their head and convince them of anything.

"You can't say anything to Grandma and Grandpa about Nanny. Remember, when we went to California, we were just visiting our friends."

I attempted to pass my history of lying onto our girls. I built a tower of babbling lies upon lies upon lies.

+ + +

How many people scoured their house and hid things before their parents arrived?

I did.

Uptight. On edge. Scared.

I examined every room to ensure not one hint of my birth mom remained obvious.

The treasured pictures of my birth mom and siblings were temporarily replaced with standby photos of other close relatives in my adoptive family.

Closets opened. Shelves scanned. Nothing apparent here.

Letters on the desk from California stuffed into drawers.

Crocheted dolls handmade for our girls forced to take a nap hidden in the bottom of the toy box.

Strict orders drilled into our girls' heads to not say a word about Nanny.

'But why, Mommy?"

"Because Grandma and Grandpa wouldn't understand. It could hurt their feelings and make them sad."

Always on guard. Always careful before I spoke. Always scanning the room for any shred of evidence while at the same time carrying on a conversation with my parents.

+ + +

One day my adoptive mom asked, "Do you keep in touch with your biological mother?"

What?

I gulped as I mulled over a response. "How did you know about that?"

"I got suspicious when you went to California. I asked your girls how many grandmas they had now. They said three. So I figured it was *her.*"

My tower of lies crumbled. My girls had not lied for me. They couldn't convince my mom with lies like I'd always been able to accomplish.

"And when are you moving to California? When were you going to tell us?"

What in the world?

This tidbit of information was only mentioned in Aunt Ann's small-town community newspaper. I thought all bases had been covered.

But someone watched my back. Someone who knew my parents. Someone who informed them of all my sneaky moves.

Chapter 24

The Soda Pop Joint

My birth mom was more like a best friend. Ten years of forming our relationship, I'm satisfied. I talked with her about topics that couldn't be discussed with my adoptive mom.

I had a mom who raised me, and a mom who gave me life and became my best friend. The best of both worlds.

But *my* world wouldn't be complete until I found my birth father.

In 1988 I again faced an intense yearning to find him. My spirit itched to fill the remaining hollowness of my roots. And the search launched once again.

With one exception this time—it will be

more complicated to accomplish, if not impossible. My mom blocked my birth father's name out of her mind, plus his name wasn't on my birth certificate, or any record, for that matter. But she remembered he paid for the medical bills, along with his physical description.

Always cautious when I mentioned my birth father, I realized my adoption was traumatic for her. I sympathized with her. Her emotions remained sensitive and seemed to still be somewhat raw.

But my desire to find him was powerful. I worried how she might respond to my selfish wish.

Might as well use what worked for me in the past—lies.

"Mom, I got a strange phone call today from a girl saying she's doing a family tree. She asked when and where I was born, asked if I was adopted, how old my mother was and if she ever lived on Raisinville Road. She said I might be related to her."

"That's odd."

"I know. She asked almost the same questions I used when searching for you."

My intent with this lie was to prompt her to start remembering him. But I didn't want her to know it was *me* who wanted to find him. I wanted it to appear like one of his kids was searching for me.

"Who do you think she was?"

"I don't know. Maybe it's one of my birth father's kids or something. Maybe they know about me."

Lies. Devious lies. My life was built on lies, but always in search of the truth.

A few weeks later I invented more lies. I attempted to pressure her enough so she'd reveal information. I prayed for her approval to search for him.

"Mom, I got another call from a guy this time. He and his sister are looking for an illegitimate baby in their family who was given up for adoption. They asked what I looked like and tried to compare physical features with their father."

"How'd they get your number?"

"I remember registering with the Michigan Search Registry back in 1978 when I searched for you. They must have gotten it from there."

"Oh, I see."

"He said they still have 10 more people to contact and he'd get back to me. If this is him, I'd really like to know. I know it's probably hard for you, but now this has me wanting to know who my father was."

"Yeah, got me wondering, too."

"Even if this isn't him…um…would you care if I tried to find him now? I don't want to hurt you, that's why I'm asking if you'd care. I actually don't know much about him. I never asked you too much before, because I knew it was hard for you. I didn't want to upset you."

"Honey, I've let bygones be bygones. Talking about him don't upset me as much as it used to. I think you should find him. You should know who your birth father is. I'll go along 200 percent with anything you come up with or want to do or want to tell anyone. I'll help you in any way I can."

My breathing quickened. Oh, my God, she gave her permission. I need to keep the pressure on before she changed her mind.

"What all do you remember?"

"I know he was engaged and she was pregnant the same time as me. When I told him I was pregnant, he took off. My dad was really mad—not at me, but at *him*. I told him your father's name and he found him. Maybe the law found him, I don't know, because it took a while. But that's when I found out from my dad that your father's girlfriend was also pregnant. But my dad made him pay for the medical bills."

"How far along was his girlfriend?"

"I have no idea. I don't think anyone ever told me."

"Anything you can remember will help."

"I lived in Dundee. I met him at a soda pop joint. I don't remember if he lived in Dundee or if he lived in Monroe and come to Dundee. I was shy and didn't ask too many questions. He used to joke with me because I was so shy. But he was a very polite guy, very well mannered. I went with him about two to three months. I didn't give in to him until the third time we was together. After I missed my first period and told him, he run off."

"Where did his girlfriend live."

"I'm not sure. But we used to stop at a little house with a picture window. It was outside of Dundee, past the school on the left side on like a slant bank. I'd wait in the car and he'd go inside for a few minutes. He told me it was his sister's house. But I learned later it was where his girlfriend lived."

"When do you remember the last time you saw him?"

"Last time I seen him was at the Monroe County Fair. He was with his wife and two kids. You know, I've growed up a lot since then, but I've forgiven a lot. I'll sign anything. You should know more of your background. I never kept nothing from you. It really eases my mind to know you want to find him. You have my total support, Sweetie. When you find him and contact him, don't hold back any feelings because he didn't have any feelings when he took off. Tell him to call me if he wants."

"Thanks, Mom."

"I'll tell you one thing, Sweetheart, I won't lie to you about any of this crap. I won't hide any of my background."

Chapter 25

Less Than Nine Months

During a visit in June 1988 with my parents in Michigan, I made up a lie about meeting an old grade-school friend for the day. We now lived in Florida. I didn't get back up north very often, so I needed to do as much "sneaky" research as possible during the few days there.

But the truth—I again stepped through the doors of my childhood library in Monroe.

"Could you please tell me where I can find the newspapers from 1953 and 1954 with the published marriages and births?"

"Right back there. It's all on microfiche. You can print copies at 25 cents per copy."

Okay, Susan. Think this through.

I was born in July 1954, which means my mom got pregnant with me in October 1953. She probably found out around November or December.

If his girlfriend was pregnant at the same time as my mom, I'll make copies of all the marriages from December 1953 to May 1954. Then copy all the births from January 1954 through October 1954.

Stay focused.

When I get back home to Florida, I'll go through to find the births that occurred in less than nine months after a marriage. Plus the marriage announcements in the newspaper give the age of the couple. I'll narrow it down even more and find the ones where the male was 17 or 18. Then I'll have some names.

My eyes sting. I'm seeing double.

Five hours later, armed with 267 copied pages, I sneaked into my parents' house and hid them in my suitcase. I had my work cut out for me.

The next two months, I dissected copies of marriages and births, trying to find matching names and dates, until they all blurred.

Seven. That's all? Seven?

Many calls to Information in Monroe, Michigan.

And, of course, more lies.

"I'm working on my family history and I'm looking for... The description I have is he was short with dark hair and dark eyes."

"No, can't be my husband. He's over six-foot tall and has blonde hair."

"Okay. Thank you."

Two more names.

I recited the details from memory.

"I'm sorry. You have the wrong person. I have green eyes and red hair."

I attempted another angle with the one remaining name.

"Hi. I'm working on my family tree. I have a picture we found in my grandmother's things, and we can't figure out who all these people are in the photo. There are some names listed on the back, and the name Jim Fitzgerald is one of them."

"That's my husband's name."

"Really? My great-aunt mentioned something about an illegitimate baby in the family being given up for adoption. She's senile, so we don't know if she's telling the truth."

"Um…I'm not sure about that. Uh…let me think. Where are you calling from?"

"I'm in Port Saint Lucie, Florida. I know the picture is from around the Dundee or Monroe area."

"Oh. My daughter lives in Melbourne, Florida. Is that near you?"

"Yes, it is. Only 40 minutes north of me."

"I tell you what. I don't want to say for sure that it's my husband in that photo. And I don't want to mention about an adoption in the family. But maybe you could take that picture to my daughter. She would know if that's her father in the picture."

"Oh, yes. I would love to do that. We're just trying to put the pieces of our family tree together."

"Here's her phone number. I'll let her know you will be calling."

+ + +

I needed my friend, Julie, for prayer support.

"Hey, Julie, do you want to ride with me to Melbourne this afternoon?"

"Sure. What's up?"

"I think I may have found my birth father. His wife acted kind of secretive and wouldn't give me much information. But I made up a story and told her I had a photo with her husband's name written on the back. Her daughter lives in Melbourne and I'm supposed to meet at her house this afternoon so she can look at the photo to see if it's her dad. I wrote a bunch of made-up names on the back of the picture, with his name being one of them."

"What? Are you nuts? What are you gonna do when she sees the photo isn't her dad?"

"It doesn't matter. I'll just say it must be someone else with the same name as her dad. I don't know. I'll make up something. I think she might be my sister. At least I'll get to meet her. If she looks like me, then I will know for sure."

"Geez, Susan, you sure get yourself into a pickle sometimes. But, yeah, I'll go with you."

We arrived at Kristen's house. While she studied the photo, I studied her face. She wasn't sure if that was her dad or not. And she didn't know any of the other people in the picture, either.

She never heard of anyone in her family being adopted or illegitimate. We chatted a short time about family trees and how difficult it is sometimes to find missing people. I thanked her for her time.

"Julie, what do you think? Did we look alike?"

"I don't know. It's hard to tell, but I don't think she's your sister."

"Oh, Julie, it has to be. It needs to be her. That was the last name on my list."

"Susan, just because you *want* it to be the right person, doesn't mean that it *is* the right one."

+ + +

Exhausting my list and not locating *him*, I read the names to my mom. Maybe she'd recognize one of them.

"I'm sorry, Honey, none of those names ring a bell at all."

"Are you sure, mom? I don't know where else to look if it's none of these guys."

+ + +

Discouraged, depressed, hopeless, I wedged papers into my bottom dresser drawer. I shoved them far back, attempting to hide them from my memory…and tears.

They silently rested, waited in darkness until January 1991, when I opened my dresser drawer in the middle of spring cleaning. I grabbed a wad of papers curled up underneath a bathing suit. I sat on my bedroom floor and flipped through the pages.

Please, God, my life won't be complete until I find him. I have to finish this search but don't know what to do next.

An idea popped into my head.

"Mom, maybe one of your teenage friends might remember his name. They might remember who you dated during the time you got pregnant with me."

"I don't know. That's a possibility."

"What are the names of your friends from back then?"

"There's George and Nancy. They got married. Their last name is Sterp. Let's see…John Testco, Harold Reagen…um…Bud Noff, and Johnny…oh, I can't remember his last name."

"That gives me a start."

"Then there was Lonny Elon, Dick Ethan, and Nancy Ticket."

I wrote as fast as she rattled off names.

"Susan, how are you gonna ever find these people?"

"I'll call Information in Dundee. Don't worry. I'll find them."

+ + +

I enlisted the help of my friend, Sue, who is an adoptee. My frazzled mind couldn't invent any more stories; it remained empty. I needed support.

I gathered phone numbers. After the first couple days, I knew the telephone conversations by heart.

"Hi. My name is Susan Beckman. My mother is Aleda Fay Pollock. She said you were friends back around 1954. Do you remember her?"

"Sure, I remember her. Very pretty girl."

"I'm trying to find someone she dated back in 1953. Do you remember a boy in town who was short? He had dark hair, dark eyes, and a big nose."

"No, can't say I recall anyone with that description. But maybe John Amel might remember. I vaguely remember she dated him for a short time."

"Do you remember a Bud Noff? Do you remember what he looked like?"

"Oh, he was tall, thin and gawky looking. He lived in Maybee. He wasn't from Dundee."

"How about a guy named Johnny?"

"Oh, yeah, Johnny Ott. He was short with dark curly hair. A wiry kid. Real nice guy."

Add names. Cross them off. The story of my life.

More names added to the page, my living room floor transformed into chaos; papers spread over the couch, the coffee table, floor and chairs.

We spent 18 hours a day inventing scenarios that could have happened. We tried finding more people on the list.

And I always gripped the cordless phone in my hand.

On day four my husband walked in the door. He stopped and laughed.

"Before long, you'll have so many papers around you, all I'll have to do is look for the phone antenna and pass your food on down."

God bless him! At least he knew how to toss some humor into a seemingly hopeless search.

Phone call after phone call. Dead ends. The names narrowed little by little.

One last name. Nancy Ticket. A phone number scribbled next to her name.

"Sue, look at the time."

"Yeah. 11:47 is too late to call anyone tonight. We'll have to wait."

"Can you come over tomorrow?"

"Of course. As soon as I get up."

We combed through papers during the next three hours, then decided we should get some rest.

Sleep didn't visit me that night. My heart ripped apart, like the shreds of paper strewn across my living room floor. I'm never gonna find my father.

I don't have a name. Not even his initials. Hopeless. Isolated.

Physically tired. Mentally worn out. Miserable. Discouraged. And still not complete as a person.

I'm never going to know anything about the other half of myself.

Chapter 26

Please Don't Hang Up

Sunday morning, January 20, 1991.

The sun still rose.

I trudged around the kitchen. Poured Diet Pepsi over the ice in my tall blue plastic cup displaying the logo, "Praise the Lord." I watched as the foam bubbled over the sides onto the orange counter. I didn't have anything to praise the Lord about. My enthusiasm died. I wanted to cry, but I'm too far gone to even allow tears to well up in my eyes.

One more name to call. The end of my search. Once Nancy Ticket denies knowing my birth father, it's done. Finished. Without a name, I had nowhere else to turn. No other road to travel. No hope to survive the brick wall I'm about to smash into.

I waited for Sue. I didn't want to call and wake her. We had been up into the early morning hours.

I stared at the walls. I twirled the fringe along the edge of the afghan around my fingers.

I watched pieces of yellow paper flutter on the floor as the ceiling fan whirled.

Swords of sunlight pierced through slats of the mini-blinds and flashed across the tan carpet.

Eight o'clock. Still no word from Sue. I couldn't wait any longer. I had to call this one last friend of my mom's.

"Nancy, this is Susan Beckman. I'm Aleda Pollock's daughter. She was a friend of yours back around 1954. Do you remember my mother?"

"Oh…kind of. I vaguely remember her when we were teenagers."

"Do you remember when she was pregnant in 1954?"

"I'm not sure if I remember her being pregnant."

"I'm trying to find my birth father."

"Well, I wouldn't know him."

"My mom can't remember his name. We thought maybe you might remember some boys she dated back then."

"I don't know how much help I'll be."

"My father was also engaged and she was pregnant the same time as my mom."

"I really don't remember her being pregnant at all. Since it's been so long ago, there's nothing I can do to help you. I'm sorry."

I envisioned her pulling the phone away from her ear. A rerun of the phone call to my aunt back in 1978.

I can't hang up the phone. She's my last chance. Now or never.

"Wait. Please don't hang up. You don't remember any names of boys she dated?"

"Where did he live?"

"My mom thinks he was either from Dundee or Monroe."

"What did he look like?"

"He was short, with dark hair, dark eyes, and a big nose"

"Well…the *only* one who fits that description is…Thurlo Wilkinson."

"What's the first name?"

"Thurlo."

I scribbled his name on a scrap of paper I snatched off the floor.

"He went with one girl for quite a while and married her. They're divorced now. I think he might have gone out with your mom a couple times."

"Do you remember where he lived?"

"I believe he was from Dundee."

"Thank you so much for your time."

He's probably not in Dundee any longer. I'm just wasting my time calling Information.

Where is Sue when I needed her?

This is useless. No need for her to hold my hand. I can survive the devastation alone.

I sighed. Stared at the name.

Wait. This doesn't make sense.

How could my mother have ever forgotten a name like Thurlo? It's not him anyway, or she would have remembered that name.

"What city, please?"

"Dundee."

"Go ahead."

"I'd like to get a phone number for Thurlo Wilkinson, please."

"The number is 313...."

A number? I have a number. He's still in Dundee after all these years? But this can't be him. It's the last person to call. I can't be that lucky.

My spirit rose. My heart sank.

Nine o'clock. My husband still slept. Sue was probably still asleep. There's no reason to get her over to my house, only to make another dead-end phone call.

I settled on making this phone call alone, but remembered God was still with me and on my side.

Chapter 27

Did You Pay?

I dialed the number.

"Hello?"

"Could I speak to Thurlo Wilkinson, please?"

"This is Thurlo."

"My name is Susan Beckman. I'm calling from Florida. I'm trying to find some of my mom's friends from back around 1953. My mom is Aleda Fay Pollock."

"Yeah. I kind of remember Fay."

"My mom was kind of short with dark brown hair and blue eyes."

"I ain't sure if I remember what she looked like."

"Do you remember when she was pregnant and gave a baby up for adoption in 1954?"

"Nope. I don't remember her being pregnant."

Getting information from him is like pulling teeth. He's not saying much. I don't have anything to lose. I'm going for it.

"I'm trying to find my birth father. He was short with dark hair, dark eyes and a big nose."

Silence. Dark silence. No response.

I can't hang up. This is the last name. I have nothing after this.

"Well, I'm the one that was adopted."

"You're the baby."

"I'm trying to find my birth father."

"I don't know who all she knew back then. I know she was seeing another guy from Monroe."

"Her father, Sanger Pollock, went after my

father and got him to pay the hospital bills."

Silence. Spooky silence. Time ceased.

He hesitated before every answer.

"Not her father."

Okay. How would he know it wasn't my grandfather who went after my father? Something is weird here.

"What?"

I raised my eyebrows at my daughters standing in the hall.

"It wasn't her father who came after him."

The only way for him to know this information would be if he is the one I'm looking for. Was it Viola who went after him?

"Were you ever approached by anyone and asked if you were the father?"

"Someone mentioned it. I was accused of it."

My daughters held their breath.

"There's no easy way to say this: Are you

the one who paid the medical bills?"

Chilling silence.

"Are you the one who paid the bills?"

"Yep…….I'm the one."

Oh, my God, what do I say now?

"After 37 years of looking for my birth father, name after name, I don't know what to say…"

"Ya know, there was another guy in Monroe. I was only with her a couple times."

"Then why did you pay the hospital bill?"

"I was planning on getting married and didn't want to get involved in a court deal."

"Was your girlfriend pregnant?"

"Yep."

My girls looked like statues.

"My mom told me that I could be my father's twin."

"Oh, really?"

"Is it possible my mom might not know who the father is?"

"It's possible."

"My mom remembers who she had sex with and who she didn't. She remembers he was short with dark hair, dark eyes and a big nose."

"Yep, that's me."

"Okay. Then what—"

"Listen, my first wife knew about this. But I'm married to my third wife now and I don't think she knows. I can't say too much because she's really the jealous type."

"I don't want to cause any trouble."

"If I done anything, I wouldn't dare let my wife know. But I do remember in '53 is when all this took place."

"Didn't you ever wonder what happened to the baby?"

"I never knew whether it was a girl or boy. And I always thought your mom had kept you."

"I have so many questions after all these years. I'm not after a paternity suit or money, nothing like that, no lawsuit. Do you mind if I ask you some questions?"

"I guess that'd be okay."

He's not much of a talker. Too much dead air between us.

"What do you look like?"

"I'm short, a little over five-four. I've got brown eyes and dark brown hair, but I use that Grecian formula on it to keep it from turning gray."

I chuckled to myself.

"Do you have other children?"

"Yep, five with my first wife. And there might be another one out there, but I ain't sure about that one."

"When was your oldest one born?"

"Mark is the oldest. He was born November 29th."

Thurlo's name appeared in the wedding

announcements in April 1954. I'd only printed out births through October 1954. If I'd only gone one month farther into November, his name would have been on my list.

My girls became aware I'd found my birth father and talking to him at that very moment. I'll never forget the smiles on their faces. I'm still not sure if they were smiles because I had completed my search, or if they were happy that they could start breathing again!

"Do your kids know about me?"

"I don't think so."

"What nationality are you?"

"German and French."

"Did you ever think about me through the years and ever wonder if I'd call?"

"Yep."

"Was it Viola who came after you to pay?"

"Viola and her husband were shady characters."

"Do you have any questions about me?"

"Nope."

"Okay. Do you mind if I call you once in a while? If your wife answers, I'll hang up. And if you answer and she's there, just tell me I have the wrong number."

"Okay."

"I don't know how much of a relationship you want. If you just want to be friends or what. It's all up to you."

"Okay."

"Do you have a picture of yourself you could send me?"

"I don't have any pictures. But I'll get one."

"I'd like that."

"What's your name and address? I need to think about this."

"My name is Susan Beckman. My address is…..if your wife finds my name, you can just tell her I was calling about some family history."

"Oh, she *won't* find this. I'll find a picture and send it to you without my wife knowing."

"Thanks, Thurlo."

I called Sue. I heard someone in a frenzy, screaming…only to realize it was me. She knew I'd found him. She was on her way out the door before she hung up the phone.

Chapter 28

Dundee Bar & Lounge

Over the next year-and-a-half, my birth father and I occasionally talked and wrote a few letters.

He's a very shy person. I always struggled to think of what to say to him. Although, he displayed a tendency towards a tender side of his personality when he'd call us in Florida during an approaching hurricane to make sure we were okay. I never determined if shyness was his nature, or maybe he was simply upset with me for finding him and barely able to tolerate me.

I learned a few things about him. He was quiet and compassionate. He drove truck for 22 years hauling sand and stone. He played guitar. He was an alcoholic.

+ + +

Then one day my adoptive mother asked, "When were you going to tell me you found your biological father?"

By now I wasn't surprised. "How did you know?"

"I have my ways. But don't ever tell your father. It would kill him."

Another time when my mom opened up for a few seconds, she mentioned, "You know, back when we adopted you, our family couldn't understand how we could love someone else's baby. So we just never talked about it."

And now I understood why adoption was never discussed in our home.

+ + +

My high school reunion approached in 1992. It was close to where Thurlo lived. If nothing else developed of our relationship, I wanted to see him in person at least one time. I reluctantly asked if we could meet. Surprisingly he agreed.

My husband didn't want to attend the reunion, so I took Sue along. We drove 1200 miles.

She was my best friend and I needed her with me, not only for emotional support, but you could say she had "the gift of gab." I was always shy and quiet. So I depended on her to keep the conversation going.

He set the meeting place, and of all places—you guessed it—a bar, which was his second home. Reaching to open the door of the Dundee Bar and Lounge, Sue grabbed my arm. She pointed to a white poster-board sign taped on the inside of the door.

Written in black Magic Marker:

Welcome to Dundee,
Susan & friend.
Love, Dad.

That's all it took to start the tears flowing. Those two words – *Love, Dad* – assured me he didn't regret that I'd found him.

The reunion with him was more emotional than I expected. Looking at his eyes, it was as if I looked in a mirror. I understood why my mother made the statement, "You look more like him than you do me."

We spent several hours together, talking and sharing our experiences in life. He told me the names of his children and where they lived. Sue wrote it down so we could search for them the next day.

We compared our feet. And, yes—I did have my father's toes!

+ + +

We figured the easiest one to find would be my sister, Stacy. She lived in Dundee. We found her address in the phone book hanging from a chain in the corner phone booth.

We circled the block. Turning the corner, peering through the kitchen window, we noticed a burly man, who appeared to be doing dishes.

"Oh, Sue. He looks mean. I don't know if we should go up to the door. What if they don't know about me? He might get mad."

"Susan, you've come this far. We're at your sister's house. The worst that can happen is they tell you to go away. This is what you came here for."

We parked in front of the house. I stumbled up the sidewalk to ring the doorbell. This burly, mean-looking man answered the door.

"I'm looking for Stacy. Is she here?"

"She's still at work."

"My name is Susan Beckman. And I'm Thurlo's daughter. I don't want to—"

"Oh, okay. Come on in."

Wait. This is the mean-looking man we just saw through the window? The one I was afraid of?

My head jerked to the right. My mouth opened, my eyebrows raised up, and a wrinkled frown popped up above my nose. Sue reacted with the same expression.

"I don't know if Stacy even knows about me. I was placed for adoption when I was three weeks old and I just found Thurlo last year and met him last night."

"Okay. Listen, Stacy won't be home until later. I'll tell her you stopped by. You could come back tomorrow night. Before you go, let me get some photo albums to look at."

Huh? This burly guy, who doesn't know me, invited me into his house, and he's freely handing over photos of the family?

I lingered over photos of Stacy and her family, committed them to memory, just in case she got mad and kicked me out of her house tomorrow.

The following night we returned. Driving down the street, I observed a pregnant woman walking alongside a toddler on a tricycle. There's my sister.

"Oh, Sue. She's outside because she's going to tell me to get out of here."

"Would you stop it and not worry about something that hasn't happened yet."

I parked the car. As I approached Stacy, she smiled. I knew she wouldn't make me leave. She invited us into her home. We talked about my adoption and about Thurlo. I explained how I found him.

"This is such a surprise. We didn't know anything about another child from Thurlo. But I'm glad you found me."

"I am, too."

"I called my older brother, Mark, and told him you were gonna be here tonight. They are driving down to meet you."

"Are you serious?"

"Yeah. He was surprised, too."

"Now, this is Mark, the brother who is four months younger than me?"

"That's right."

"Crazy, isn't it?"

Stacy's daughter wanted to go back outside to catch lightning bugs. We sat on the stoop of her front porch. A car turned the corner and parked in the driveway.

"That's Mark and his wife, Darlene."

My stomach bubbled. My heart missed a few beats.

Was he going to be mad at me?

He skipped around the corner of the house, walked up to me with a wide smile and open arms.

"Damn. I always thought I was the oldest one."

What an exciting way to be welcomed into their family.

"I didn't know if you guys would want to have a relationship with me or not. I don't want to cause any trouble with your mom."

"Hey, Sis, whatever Thurlo and our mom did back then had nothing to do with us. If we want to get to know you, that's up to us and our decision. It doesn't involve them."

Mark called their other brother, Brian. He worked at the mall in Ypsilanti in a shoe store. Brian wanted to meet me, too. Stacy was tired and stayed home that night, but the rest of us drove the 30 miles to meet Brian. He greeted me with a tight hug. Then we drove to his apartment.

I spent the next few hours beginning another new relationship with another extended family.

Chapter 29

Saying Good-Bye

Over the next five years, I learned more about Thurlo. He spoke of me often to his family and friends. He freely showed people my pictures and cards. He often carried my letters with him.

He was very proud of the afghan I made for him. If he wasn't using it (which wasn't very often), he proudly displayed it. He wanted to visit us in Florida, but had never flown and was leery.

He had a hard life—some of it he created for himself—some of it others created. He was a very sensitive person. He could not handle life's curves. He could not deal with problems well. Thus, he escaped into the bottle.

He was a very shy, introverted person. He never quite figured out how to relate to his children. In the end, he was ashamed of who he had become.

At times he could be stubborn.

Now I know where I get my stubbornness from.

And like most of us, he was aware of his faults and mistakes, but he was unable to go back in time and correct them. He didn't have much confidence in himself.

He enjoyed hearing from all of his children, be it a visit, card, pictures or letters. He was ashamed of his writing and spelling. It would take him months to compose even a small note.

He suffered much guilt when it came to his children. There was so much he wanted to say, but had no idea how to put it in words.

At last he is at peace.

+ + +

Thurlo Gavana Wilkinson passed away on September 10, 1997.

I met him one time to say hello. We met a second time to say good-bye.

While flying from Florida to Michigan, I wrote my thoughts to speak at his memorial service on September 20, 1997. I rewrote this several times, only because my tears kept smearing the ballpoint pen writing on the blue legal pad paper, and I didn't care if other passengers on the plane saw me crying.

His memorial service was in Tecumseh, Michigan, the small town where my adoptive parents lived. I sat in the back seat of my sister's car. As they drove through town, I scanned people in cars, praying that my parents wouldn't pull up beside us at the next red stop light. I'm fearful they might see me in the parking lot of the church.

I didn't know how I could lie my out of appearing in Michigan when I lived in Florida.

Always on guard. Afraid.

Before his memorial service, I only knew my sister and two brothers. But now I had this opportunity to meet the rest of the family. I was welcomed with open arms.

I chuckled...I also had never been in a roomful of people whose side view mimicked my big nose!

Some of us read our memorial thoughts about Thurlo. With tears, I blubbered through mine:

> *Some of you here today may not know who I am. In fact, Thurlo did not know me until exactly six years and eight months ago, when I first contacted him by telephone.*
>
> *After searching 37 years for my birth father, I finally found him on January 20, 1991, when I talked to Thurlo for the first time.*
>
> *I did not know what to expect when I found him, nor did I have any great expectations. Therefore, I was not disappointed, and just accepted him as he was.*
>
> *I had not been looking for a father figure, because I already had two wonderful parents whom had adopted me as an infant and raised me.*
>
> *I had been searching for my roots, my heredity, my past family and medical history. As an adoptee, maybe I wanted these answers for my own selfish reasons of feeling connected to some blood kin.*

I did not want anything from Thurlo except that information. But instead, I found a friend. I found a lonely man, feeling guilty for all the wrong he had done in the past.

Thurlo and I met only one time (of course, in a bar) and spent only a few hours talking. But since that time five years ago, we kept in touch with phone calls, letters and pictures. I will especially miss his phone calls to check on me when a hurricane is heading towards Florida.

Although we never had any real serious, deep conversations, I am thankful to God for at least the opportunity to share just the simple everyday events with Thurlo.

I was thinking the other day that even though he definitely had rough times in his life, and might not have always made the right decisions, if it weren't for Thurlo, I wouldn't be here; I wouldn't have two lovely daughters, and most importantly my beautiful granddaughter, Brittney.

God did not break His promise to me that I would know my heritage.

And I promise to God that I will pass on, to my children and grandchildren, the genealogical history of Thurlo Gavana Wilkinson.

Chapter 30

The End – Or So I Thought

I can only thank God and give Him all the glory, praise, and credit for opening the doors along the way of my search. I know under my own power, I could have never orchestrated any type of organized plan to find my birth family.

Then 41 years after my birth, God still opened doors—even though I was pleased with the end of my search, God revealed He was going to allow something more to happen.

+ + +

In October 1995, I had the privileged opportunity to meet Jett Williams. She is the birth daughter of Hank Williams, Sr., born just five days after he passed away. She shared her adoption story, and the frustration and obstacles involved with her adoption and proving paternity.

The wheels in my mind starting turning. Jett was just the inspiration I needed to take the final step in having my "original" birth certificate "amended." I never knew anyone accomplishing this step.

+ + +

"Thurlo, I'd like to ask a favor. My original birth certificate doesn't have the name of my father. Would you be willing to sign some papers so I can get your name put on there?"

"Even though I'd done bad in the past and regret a lot of things, I'd be honored to have my name on your birth certificate, because I'm proud to be your father. I'll sign anything you need."

> Paperwork.
> Applications.
> Letters.
> Affidavits.
> Notarized forms.

Mail. Mail. Mail. Back and forth. Copies mailed to state departments.

What do you mean you don't have the affidavits I mailed you? How could you lose them?

The End – Or So I Thought

Imagine, government offices losing important paperwork!

If it wasn't for Jett's story of her persistence, I wouldn't have been motivated to continue my path of fighting the system.

More months of mail. Back and forth.

After three years of nothing more than red tape, in the summer of 1998, I opened the envelope which contained my "amended original" birth certificate. Black and white—for the first time—my birth father's name—on my birth certificate—connected to me.

I thank God that the signatures needed from Thurlo were obtained before his death.

He passed away before the final certificate was certified and issued. Sadly, he never had the opportunity to see his name on my birth certificate. Therefore, I not only needed to accomplish this fight and challenge with the system for my own benefit, but also, in memory of my birth father.

Chapter 31

Me

I now achieved closure to the last chapter of my adopted life. I don't ever need to go back into the past and search for answers that aren't there. I can look forward now and get on with my life.

> No more questions.
> No more doubts.
> No more emptiness.
>
> I am complete.
> I know where I came from.

I can now, once and for all, look in the mirror and never again question who I look like. I can now give any doctor my *entire* medical background.

And the question of *WHY* is answered. The

one-word question that haunts every adoptee.

But you know what? Once you find out the answers, the reason *why* just doesn't seem all that important anymore. What is important is to feel complete and whole as a person. I finally have roots and heredity. The days of discouragement and defeat seem like they happened in another lifetime.

Actually, it was another lifetime…

It was before I found ME!

Susan Marie Angela Pollock Wilkinson Clum Beckman

Epilogue

1995: I always wondered if it is true that I had been sick after I was taken from my birth mom. I wanted to believe her story, but it was hard to imagine. Out of curiosity, I wrote the hospital requesting medical records under the name of Susan Marie Pollock for July and/or August 1954.

I received records.

And yes, it was true.

1999: In 1978 when I requested nonidentifying information, I was given only my amended adoptive name, date of birth, and adoptive parents' names.

In 1999, I learned that the Michigan Adoption Law regarding Release of Information had been revised and expanded. I requested information again from the courthouse. The following nonidentifying information was in my file all along.

It wasn't released to me until I was 45 years old:

> *You were born on July 18, 1954, at Florence Crittenton Home in Jackson, Michigan. At birth you weighed 5 pounds 2.5 ounces and were 18 inches long. There were no complications at birth and no feeding difficulties. The length of labor was 4 hours. At the time of your birth, your first name was Susan.*
>
> *At the time of your birth your birth mother was 17 years old and single. She was of Irish-Dutch and American Southern ancestry and her religious preference was Protestant. It appears your birth mother lived with her mother until she was killed in a car accident. Upon the death of her mother, her father was then appointed guardian of your birth mother and her 3 siblings. It appears your birth*

mother lived in different boarding homes and relatives prior to her commitment to the Florence Crittenton Home.

Your birth mother voluntarily terminated her parental rights. It should be noted that since she was a minor, her father also had to consent to the voluntary termination of her parental rights.

You were placed with your adoptive family on August 9, 1954. It appears you were at the Florence Crittenton Home until your placement with your adoptive family.

2013: I look back at my life and wonder how things could have been different. I think the only thing I would have liked changed was the communication with my adoptive parents.

Everything else was wonderful. My parents were great. I pray I didn't portray them as not good parents just because they wouldn't talk about adoption.

I'd like to offer a few suggestions to each

member of the adoption triad, based on my personal experience, in the following pages.

You might agree or disagree. Every adoption is different. Every family is different. Take some suggestions to heart, throw away the rest. Use what works best for your family situation.

I could go on and on with more suggestions, more feelings, more "do this" and "don't do that," which could turn into another book!

But I tried to keep it short.

For Adoptees

Try to open the communication with your adoptive parents. Reassure them you do not want to replace them. Be sensitive to your adoptive parents' feelings. If they won't communicate, don't push it.

Join a search and support group. This helped me tremendously. I finally found others like me.

Keep in touch with the agency, court, and/or attorney who facilitated the adoption. Keep your contact information updated. Keep a Waiver of Confidentiality updated. This way if anyone in your birth family is searching for you, the agency has permission to release your information to them.

Become proactive in support of changing the laws regarding closed adoption records. Most members of the adoption triad agree that adoption records should be opened to the adoptee at age 18.

Remember, when you find your birth parent, the last image they have of you is most likely as an infant. In their mind you haven't grown up. Give them their time to treat you as a child at first, until they've adjusted to you as an adult.

Be prepared for any scenario, no matter how bizarre it might seem. You never know what you will find at the end of your search. Once you've imagined almost every possibility, then you will pretty much be prepared for anything.

During the time of your search, you've had a chance to get used to the idea of eventually finding your birth parent. Keep in mind that when you do find, the birth parent is usually taken by surprise because they haven't had the same length of time to prepare for a reunion, like you have.

Read every book you can get your hands on regarding adoption. Share these books with your adoptive parents, your spouse, your children, your friends. Read books written by all members of the adoption triad. Learn how other adoptees feel as they get older. Learn about the struggles a birth mother goes through, regardless whether she voluntarily placed you for adoption or whether you were involuntarily taken from her for various reasons. Be aware of what other adoptive parents have experienced.

For Birth Parents

Read. Read. Read. Read every book you can get your hands on regarding adoption. Read books written by all members of the adoption triad. This will give you insight as to what other birth parents, your child and adoptive parents go through.

Hook up with a support group. You'll be surprised you aren't alone with your experiences and emotions.

Become proactive in support of changing the laws regarding closed adoption records. Most members of the adoption triad agree that adoption records should be opened to the adoptee at age 18.

Keep in touch with the agency, court, and/or attorney who facilitated the adoption. Keep your contact information updated. Keep a Waiver of Confidentiality updated. This way if anyone in your child's family is searching for you, the agency has permission to release your information to them.

Write letters and send pictures to be placed in your child's file. If your child comes searching for you, they will be reassured that you did think about them through the years.

Keep your medical history updated in the file. Most likely you did not have any major illness or disease at the time of adoption. These usually occur later in life. If you don't update this information, your child will never know what is hidden in their family medical history.

When reuniting, be prepared for your child to not immediately become attached to your side. Give them time.

Don't assume they will change their life to satisfy your wishes of what could be.

Be prepared for the possibility they won't accept you as a "mom" or "dad," but you could end up becoming their best friend.

For Adoptive Parents

Keep the line of communication open with your child. Yes, life does go on after adoption. But be open minded. Let your child share their feelings. Then encourage them to talk about adoption. If they don't want to talk about it, maybe have them write a letter to their birth parents. They might not talk for fear of hurting you.

You might not like the idea of them finding their birth parents one day, but that possibility does come attached to an adoption. Don't be afraid that your child wants to replace you and run back to their birth family. That thought might cut through your heart like a sword.

If you've raised your child the best you know how, they won't walk away from you. Help them with their search. Tell them that when the right time comes, you will walk by their side. They need support from somewhere and what better place than from the only parents they've ever known.

Even if you know the birth parents might never be found, just tell them you will help in any way possible. Let them be the one to search, whether there's a birth parent at the end of the dream rainbow or not.

I felt I was forced to lie in order to find the truth.

If my parents would have been open, I probably wouldn't have told one lie. The secrecy involved made me feel like a criminal. Shameful. Guilty. I felt like a commodity that was sold and bought. I exceled in trying to make my parents happy with the product they purchased.

Be aware that your child did have a prior history before adoption. I've often thought: When you get married, you accept your spouse's family which come attached to them, whether you like it or not. Your in-laws become your extended family. Why can't it be the same with adoptees? They had a family they came from. Why can't adoptive parents accept that as an extended family for their child?

My advice to adoptive parents is to read, read, read. Read every book you can get your hands on regarding adoption. Read books written by all members of the adoption triad. Become knowledgeable regarding how your child will feel as they get older. Learn about the struggles a birth mother goes through, regardless whether she voluntarily placed her baby for adoption or whether the baby was involuntarily taken from her for various reasons. Be aware of what other adoptive parents have experienced. How others have helped their child walk through emotional ups and downs.

Share these books with your child at an appropriate age. Get them to read, read, read. They will gain insight into the lives of other adoptees. Every story is different, but the void is always there. The feeling of being different could be lessened when they learn that other adoptees carry the same emotions and questions.

Back in the 1950s, adoptive parents were not told anything about how their baby would feel later on in life. Agencies often lied about the baby's birth parents, such as having very high IQs. Adoptive parents felt they needed to excel in their parenting skills, otherwise if the child turns out not so good, they might be labeled as bad parents. They forget about what lurks in the genes of the child.

Medical history of birth parents doesn't exist at the time of adoption, because what young person has any major medical problems? Most diseases don't surface until later in life. If I would not have found my birth parents, I would never know that my birth father died at age 62 from cancer or that my birth mother had breast cancer and died at age 72. This is why I feel records need to be opened. Laws are changing all the time. I realize things are different now than they were back in the 1950s.

Support groups are an excellent avenue for everyone to become connected to others "like them." I never knew another adoptee until age 24. When your child is young, find another adopted child for them to be friends with. At the same time you might also find for yourself an adoptive parent to share with.

In the search and support group I co-founded, some adoptees attended the meetings with their adoptive parents playing an active role in the search. I know at times it was hard. But at the end of the search, the adoptee was able to share their excitement and joy with their parents. I never had that chance.

More adoptive parents should become proactive in support of changing the laws regarding the secrecy of adoption records. Most members of the adoption triad agree that adoption records should be opened to the adoptee at age 18.

I never liked to be put on a pedestal as the Special Chosen One. I just wanted to blend in with the rest of the family. My case might be different since I grew up with a sister who wasn't adopted. I think it also made her feel uncomfortable since she was born into the family and my brother and I were singled out as the special ones. I never wanted her to feel left out. Treat your adopted child the same as one born into your family.

Write letters and send pictures to be placed in your child's file. If anyone from your child's birth family is searching, they will be comforted to know they weren't forgotten through the years.

Acknowledgments

First of all, I give all the praise and glory to my Lord and God, Jesus Christ. He gave me my first breath. He infused in me the genetics of my birth family. He placed me in an exceptionally loving and nurturing adoptive home. He covered me with His wings through the years and protected me more than I will ever know.

Second, I thank my dear husband, Greg. God knew what He was doing when He put us together. You stood by me all these years, even when I didn't deserve it. You deserve a medal for sticking around through my highs and lows and in-betweens. You also covered me with your love and affection, your protection, and kept me from going over the edge many times; otherwise, I don't know where I would be today.

I thank my daughters, Amy and Wendy, for tolerating my craziness and irrationalism in your lifetime, especially during the times of my searches. I pray that my life experiences can be lessons for you and your children. I pray you both find comfort and peace under God's wings.

I thank my two dogs, Miya and Zee, for forcing me to walk away from my computer, when you would unceasingly bark and bark until I would let you outside. Tending to be a workaholic, I probably wouldn't have taken any breaks if it weren't for my two *furry* girls.

I thank the girls in my Faith-Builders Critique Group for your loving, constructive criticism; for bearing with me from the beginning with my very *raw* rough drafts; thanks for your friendship and prayers.

I thank my friend of 40 years, Teresa Dallas, in Evansville, Indiana, for helping me clear my mind and suggesting book titles…and for always reminiscing with me.

I thank Lar Sinclair, from Sinclair PhotoGraphic Design, in Chesaning, Michigan, for sharing your fabulous expertise in helping design this awesome book cover.

I thank my deceased birth mother for giving me life. You did not reject me when I found you. You became my best friend. Thanks for being open with me when I searched for my birth father. We shared a lot through the years before God took you home. I always loved you, even before I found you. And thanks for the crooked smile!

I thank my deceased birth father for admitting the truth, not rejecting me and for beginning a relationship with me as an adult. The few years we shared before God took you home are deeply cherished. I know you are now at peace. Oh, and by the way, thanks for the big nose!

I thank my 12 half-siblings; some for accepting me unconditionally into their families; some choosing not to accept me. I love you all.

I thank my deceased adoptive parents for relentlessly pursuing adoption until God ultimately blessed you with me. I thank you for your patience, your upright moral lifestyle, and discipline. I wish we could have talked more regarding my adoption, but I understand your fears of doing so in that era. I always wanted to thank you for adopting me. I wouldn't have wished for anything different. You were wonderful parents.

My heredity from my birth parents, combined with the loving environment of my adoptive parents, all according to God's plan, have shaped me into the person I am today.

READING GROUP QUESTIONS

1. What did you know about adoptees' feelings before reading *The Special Chosen One*? How did this book teach you, or change your impression, about the obstacles encountered by adoptees?

2. Is there anything Susan could have done differently to open communication with her adoptive parents regarding adoption and her search?

3. Do you think adoption records should be open to adoptees and/or birth parents when the adoptee turns 18? Why or why not?

4. What do you think of how Susan's siblings reacted when they found out they had a sister and wanted a relationship despite the birth mother and birth father?

5. Why is it important for adoptees to feel complete and whole as a person? Do people not adopted have these same issues?

6. How do you think Susan would have reacted if her birth parents had rejected her at the end of the search?

7. What was the major theme of *The Special Chosen One*? What did you learn from this book?

TIPS TO BEGIN SEARCHING

1. Get Organized. Keep a diary. Keep a correspondence index. Keep a research chart.

2. Start at the Beginning. Talk to adoptive parents. Learn place of adoption. Be prepared for every kind of scenario.

3. State Laws. Know your state law before beginning search. Laws change every day.

4. Registries. Register with International Soundex Reunion Registry, state agency (if available), and other agencies found on line.

5. Letters. Write to agency, court, state, etc., to request nonidentifying information and waiver of confidentiality.

6. Public Records. Wills and probates. State board of corporations. Vessels and aircraft. Telephone directories. State licensing board. City directories. Real estate records. Churches. Divorce, marriage and death records. Voter registration.

7. Obituaries.

8. Bureau of Indian Affairs.

9. Search and Support Groups.

10. Read. Read. Read.

    More detailed information can be found in my booklet *10 Critical Guidelines to Begin Searching for Your Birth Family*.

RECOMMENDED READING

10 Critical Guidelines to Begin Searching for Your Birth Family – Susan Beckman

360 Square: A Memoir of Adoption and Identity – Carol Lillieqvist Welsh

A Face Like Mine: A Memoir – Eleanor Church, Chris Fitz, Clive Matson, Sally Aberg

The Adopted Break Silence – Jean Paton

Adopted Reality, A Memoir – Laura Dennis

An Adopted Woman – Katrina Maxtone-Graham

Adoptee Trauma – Heather Carlini

Adoption and Loss – The Hidden Grief – Evelyn Robinson

Adoption Detective: Memoir of an Adopted Child – Judith Land and Martin Land

Adoption Encounter – Mary Jo Rillera

Adoption Forum: Intimate Discussions to Unite the Triad in Healing – Kasey Hamner

Adoption Healing…A Path to Recovery – Joe Soll

Adoption Maze: An Adoptee's True Struggle Finding Herself – Truth Justice

The Adoption Reader: Birth Mothers, Adoptive Mothers and Adopted Daughters Tell Their Stories – Wadia Ells

Adoption Reunions: A Book for Adoptees, Birth Parents and Adoptive Families – Michelle McColm

The Adoption Reunion Handbook – Elizabeth Trinder, Julia Feast, David Howe

Adoption Reunion Stories – Shirley Budd Pusey

The Adoption Reunion Survival Guide: Preparing Yourself for the Search, Reunion and Beyond – Julie Jarrell Bailey and Lynn N. Giddens

Adoption Searchbook, The – Mary Jo Rillera

Adoption Triangle, The – Annette Baran, Reuben Pannor, Arthur D. Sorosky

Akin to the Truth: A Memoir of Adoption and Identity – Paige Strickland

Are You My Mommy? The Search for My Birth Mother – Janet Louise Stephenson

Back to the Beginning; Remarkable True Stories of Adoption Searches & Reunions – Ava Friddle, Judy Andrews, Kristen Hamilton, Joe Bardin

Because I Loved You: A Birthmother's View of Open Adoption – Patricia Dischler

Becoming Patrick: A Memoir – Patrick McMahon

Being Adopted: The Lifelong Search for Self – Schechter & Henig Brodzinsky

Birth Bond: Reunions Between Birthparents & Adoptees – Judith Gediman & Linda P. Brown

Birthright: The Guide to Search and Reunion for Adoptees, Birth Parents and Adoptive Parents – Jean Strauss

Black Market Baby: An Adopted Woman's Journey – Renee Clarke

Call Me Ella – Joan E. Kaufman

Circles: One Woman's 30-Year Search For Her Birth Family – Jan Wiseman

Coffee & Cake: An Adoptee in Search of Her Past – Julia I. Meyers

Dear Birthmother, Thank You for Our Baby – Kathleen Silber & Phylis Speedlin

Faces of Adoption – E. Lynn Giddens

Family: An Open Adoption Adventure – Sandy Kelly

Family Secrets: A Writer's Search for His Parents & His Past – David Leitch

Finding Dolores II: Beyond Search and Reunion – Thomas Muldary

Finding Family: My Search for Roots and the Secrets in My DNA – Richard Hill

Finding Gloria – Marianne Curtis

Following the Tambourine Man: A Birthmother's Memoir – Janet Mason Ellerby

Found: A Memoir – Jennifer Lauck

Full Circle: Lost and Found in the Ring of Adoption – Virginia Hunt Tuft

Giving Away Simone – Jan Waldron

Halfway Home: Contact & Reunion Guidelines – Lynn-Claire Davis

How It Feels to be Adopted – Jill Krementz

Ithaka: A Daughter's Memoir of Being Found – Sarah Saffian

I'm Still Me – Betty Jean Lifton

In Search of A Stranger – Warren E. Siegmond

I Would Have Searched Forever – Sandy Musser

Jessica Lost: A Story of Birth, Adoption & The Meaning of Motherhood – Bunny Crumpacker, J.S. Picariello

Journey of the Adopted Self – Betty Jean Lifton

Letters From the Heart – Sandy Musser

Letter to Louise: A Loving Memoir to the Daughter I Gave Up for Adoption More Than Twenty-Five Years Ago – Pauline Collins

Lost: Woman, Found: Child (A Memoir): Becoming The Woman I am by Searching for the Child I Never Was – J. Page Jones

Love Child – Sue Elliott

Love Your Mother, Like It or Not – Jim Sutherland

Lucky Girl: A Memoir – Mei-Ling Hopgood

Mamalita: An Adoption Memoir – Jessica O'Dwyer

My Own Legacy: An Adoption Memoir – Katie McMillan

My Third Parents: Orphanage to an American Dream – Fernando Kuehnel

On the Outside Looking In – Michael Reagan & Joe Hyams

One Perfect Day: A Mother and Son's Journey of Adoption and Reunion – Diane Burke

One Small Sacrifice: A Memoir: Lost Children of the Indian Adoption Projects – Trace A. DeMeyer

Orphan Voyage – Jean Paton

The Pieces Come Together…At Last: The Memoirs of an Adult Adoptee and Her Sister – Patricia A. Walsh, Arlene P. Loucks

Primal Wound, The – Nancy Verrier

Reunion Book, The – Mary Jo Rillera

Search For Anna Fisher – A. Florence Fisher

Searching for Jane, Finding Myself - Jan Fishler

Second-Chance Mother: A Memoir of Adoption, Loss and Reunion – Denise Roessle

Second Choice: Growing Up Adopted – Robert Anderson

Secret Storms: A Mother and Daughter, Lost then Found – Julie Mannix von Zerneck, Kathy Hatfield

A Single Square Picture: A Korean Adoptee's Search for Her Roots – Katy Robinson

Soul Connection: Memoir of A Birthmother's Healing Journey – Ann H. Hughes

Split at the Root: A Memoir of Love and Lost Identity – Catana Tully

Sunlight on My Shadow – Judy Liautaud

Swimming Up the Sun: A Memoir of Adoption – Nicole Burton

Swing, the Search for My Birth Father, Louis Prima – Alan Gerstel

Synchronicity and Reunion: The Genetic Connection of Adoptees and Birthparents – LaVonne H. Stiffler

That Picture of You: A Dramatic Real-Life Story of Adoption and Reunion – Susan J. Bevan

The Girls Who Went Away – Ann Fessler

The Other Mother – Carol Schaefer

The Third Floor – Judi Loren Grace

This is My Lemonade: An Adoption Story – Robert Mulkey

Thread of Life: An Adoption Story – Mike Doiron

To Prison With Love – Sandy Musser

Twice Born: Memoirs of an Adopted Daughter – Betty Jean Lifton

Two Hearts: An Adoptee's Journey Through Grief to Gratitude – Linda Hoye

What Kind of Love is This – Sandy Musser

When God Intervenes – Dabney Hedegard

Where Are My Birth Parents? – Karen Gravelle & Susan Fisher

Which Mother is Mine? – Joan Oppenheimer

Who Gives Up Adorable Little Girls Anyway? The Search for My Birth Father – Janet Louise Stephenson

Who is My Mother – Clare Marcus

Without A Map: A Memoir – Meredith Hall

HELPFUL LINKS

ADOPTEE-BIRTHPARENT SUPPORT NETWORK
http://adopteebirthparentsupportnetwork.org

ADOPTEES' SUPPORT FORUM
http://www.adopting.org/ffcwnr.html

ADOPTION DATABASE
http://www.adoptiondatabase.org

ADOPTION HEALING
https://www.adoptionhealing.com

ADOPTION REUNION REGISTRY
http://registry.adoption.com

ADOPTION SEARCH & REUNION
http://reunion.adoption.com

ADOPTION SEARCH & REUNION SUPPORT
GROUPS IN CANADA
http://www.familyhelper.net/ft/ftsup.html

ADOPTION TRACKER
http://www.adoptiontracker.com

ALMA (Adoptees' Liberty Movement Association)
http://almasociety.org

AMERICAN ADOPTION CONGRESS
http://www.americanadoptioncongress.org/search_faq.php

HOW TO INVESTIGATE
http://www.howtoinvestigate.com/adoption.htm#.UnqSdOLNKMM

INTERNATIONAL SOUNDEX REUNION REGISTRY
http://www.isrr.net/registration.shtml

PIECES OF DREAMS REGISTRY
http://www.angelfire.com/folk/piecesofdreams

STATE STATUTES SEARCH
https://www.childwelfare.gov/systemwide/laws_policies/state/index.cfm?event=stateStatutes.showSearchForm

YAHOO ADOPTION SEARCH & REUNION GROUPS
http://groups.yahoo.com/neo/dir/1600768591

Please note: Some of the above web site addresses may have changed since publication.

My birth mom pregnant with me in 1954

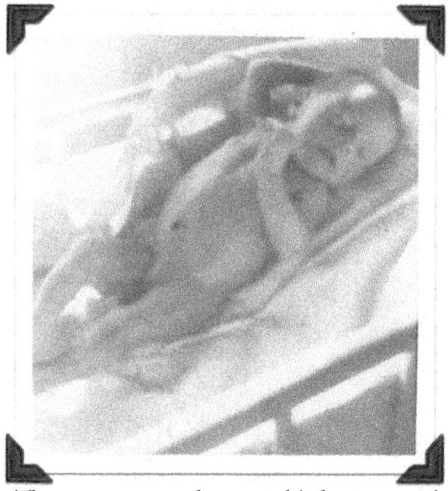

The one nursery photo my birth mom took
of me as a newborn
July 1954

My birth mom holding me for the last time
before I was taken to foster care.
Note the expression of the nurse in the background
and the open car door waiting for me.

My parents and me in 1955

My parents, brother & sister
1960

My parents at our Wedding
April 1973

My parents, brother & sister
2000

My birth mom in 1976

My birth mom & her husband, Bill

The only picture I have of our airport reunion
November 1978

Reunited in November 1978

Aunt Ann, Uncle Hank & Me
1978

Aunt Ann & Me
November 1978

Aunt Ann, Birth Mom & Me
Newspaper picture
November 1978

My birth father
July 1992

Me & my Birth Father
Reunited in July 1992

Meeting my birth father in 1992
with the sign he taped to the bar door

Dundee Bar & Lounge

My birth father
Shortly before he passed away

My Daddy, Marissa & Wendy
September 2008

My Mom & Me
May 2011

My husband & Me
December 2012

Our girls, Wendy & Amy
October 2013

Our three oldest grandchildren
Marissa, Brittney, Spencer
March 2013

Our youngest granddaughter, Alaira
November 2013

Me & my Mom 2010   Birth Mom & Me 1978

ABOUT THE AUTHOR

Susan Beckman is a Christian and a writer.

Susan is an adoptee who searched and found both birth parents in 1978 and 1992. She was co-founder of a search and support group for adoptees, birth families and adoptive parents, *Mother and Child Reunion.* She has helped many people search and find each other.

Susan has published *10 Critical Guidelines to Begin Searching for Your Birth Family* and *The Unforgettable Angel.* She has published short stories in newsletters, booklets, newspapers, and magazines, such as *Breakthrough Intercessor, Victory Herald, Living Stones News, Christian Citizen USA* and *City Light News.*

Susan was born and raised in Michigan and met her husband in high school in Ohio, where they married in 1973. They have lived in Florida since 1982.

They have two daughters and four grandchildren. She is blessed to have them living nearby, giving her the pleasure to be actively involved and participate in their lives, both socially and spiritually.

Susan lives in the country and enjoys decorating their home in old-fashioned farmhouse style. In addition to reading and writing, she enjoys Bible studies, quilting, candlemaking, herbology, cooking, canning, genealogy, crocheting, knitting, spinning and gardening.

She would love to hear from you!

Email: sbeckmanauthor@aol.com
Web site: www.susanbeckman.com
FaceBook: https://www.facebook.com/SusanBeckmanAuthor
Twitter: @beckman

www.ingramcontent.com/pod-product-compliance
Lightning Source LLC
LaVergne TN
LVHW041608070426
835507LV00008B/171